CHOOSING JOY

ANGELA THOMAS

CHOOSING

A 52-WEEK DEVOTIONAL FOR
DISCOVERING TRUE HAPPINESS

 HOWARD BOOKS
A DIVISION OF SIMON & SCHUSTER, INC.

NEW YORK   NASHVILLE   LONDON   TORONTO   NEW DELHI

Howard Books
A Division of Simon & Schuster, Inc.
1230 Avenue of the Americas
New York, NY 10020

First Howard Books trade paperback edition December 2011

HOWARD and colophon are trademarks of Simon & Schuster, Inc.

For information about special discounts for bulk purchases, please contact Simon & Schuster Special Sales at 1-866-506-1949 or business@simonandschuster.com.

The Simon & Schuster Speakers Bureau can bring authors to your live event. For more information or to book an event contact the Simon & Schuster Speakers Bureau at 1-866-248-3049 or visit our website at www.simonspeakers.com.

Designed by Davina Mock-Maniscalco

Manufactured in the United States of America

10 9 8 7 6 5 4 3 2 1

Library of Congress Cataloging-in-Publication Data
Thomas, Angela.
    Choosing joy / Angela Thomas.
        p. cm.
    1. Joy—Biblical teaching.   2. Joy—Religious aspects—Christianity—Textbooks.
    I. Title.
BS680.J6T46   2011
241'.4—dc23   2011033580
ISBN 978-1-4391-6581-2
ISBN 978-1-4516-2887-6 (ebook)

For
Joe Thomas
I love you, Daddy.
Thank you for always choosing joy.

Contents

Introduction

Hello, my friends,

I am so grateful to welcome you to this year-long devotional, *Choosing Joy*. I have been praying for you as I have studied and written. I am asking God to meet you in the words of these pages to give you fresh encouragement and strength. As far as I can tell, we are some of the busiest people on the planet, in the busiest days any generation has ever known. And if there was ever a time we needed to intentionally choose joy, it's now.

For that very reason, we've designed this year of *Choosing Joy* into bite-size morsels. On Mondays, I'll introduce a new Bible passage and new study-focus for that week. The next four days will take the focus a little deeper and wider. Each day is meant to be small enough to fit into your crowded life, but sturdy enough to challenge you spiritually. We've included lines for each day (I love lines!) because we'd love for you to take the time to apply these short truths to your everyday life. We've even added some extra journaling pages at the back of the book for those days when your words just overflow.

I really want to encourage you to write. I believe that in your actual writing and praying, God is going to do so much more than I could ever do. If you're afraid of someone reading your pages, then write in code! Or draw pictures. Or just write enough to remind yourself how God is speaking to your heart. Sometimes the very process of putting your thoughts down on paper is the action forcing you to think about what's happening inside of you. Sometimes you will even write thoughts and insights you didn't even know you had.

I have written this devotional as a word study. That means I have spent months tracking the word *joy* and all its variations through the Scriptures. I know that I am changed forever because of these months. I have also tried to stay true to the Bible's use of the word by writing directly from the intent of each passage and not just my own experiences. This book focuses on choosing joy, as we understand it from the Scriptures, which is many times different than how this world has taught us to define joy.

May this be the year that God supernaturally transforms your heart. May these days of study radically change your very nature. God has promised that His Word will not return void. Your commitment to learn from these small studies centered on joy will not leave you the same. I know that God will use His Word to give, restore and multiply His joy in your heart.

And so, dear one, let this new year of joy begin in your life and mine.

Angela

CHOOSING JOY

WEEK I

For the Glory of God

THE PURSUIT OF JOY

*Then I will go to the altar of God, to God, my **joy** and my delight.*
—Psalm 43:4

*Not that we lord it over your faith, but we work with you for your **joy**.*
—2 Corinthians 1:24

As we begin this year of intentionally choosing joy, I want us to begin with one purpose in mind. We must choose joy in our everyday lives because a joy-filled life brings glory to God. God shines brightly through the soul that is wholly devoted to Him. Satisfied in Him. Trusting in Him. Delighting in Him.

If the pursuit of joy has seemed too worldly to you, then I pray this year of Scripture-directed joy will change your heart. The pursuit of joy and the glory of God are not in conflict. In fact, just the opposite is true. To pursue joy with your whole life is to honor the One who has given you life.

Would you let this truth release you into a year of running

hard after all the joy God has for you through Jesus Christ? There is no guilt in pursuing joy on this earth. To turn away from this pursuit is to turn away from an opportunity to glorify God.

As you will see in the months to come, the pursuit of joy is a significant endeavor. For any man or woman who takes spiritual maturity seriously, the pursuit of joy must become a priority. Joy in your everyday life will not always be the comfortable kind of joy we have grown accustomed to in our culture. Pursuing joy in God is very different from just enjoying His gifts. Most of us know how to enjoy His gifts. But the pursuit of joy actually transforms us from the inside out.

Through His Word and our pursuit, His power and our surrender, the Creator of joy can put His joy inside of us. He can create in us what we have not been able to manufacture on our own. The more we approach the throne of God for this transformation, the more of God we will encounter. God desires that we would find our joy, our happiness, our peace, and our purpose in Him. When we have done so, He is glorified.

Through these weeks of devotion, we'll pursue His joy together. May we cherish this journey and the joy that is set before us. May we pray with the psalmist: *"O God, you are my God; earnestly I seek you; my soul thirsts for you; my body longs for you, in a dry and weary land where there is not water"* (Psalm 63:1).

Now, write your own prayer about seeking the joy of the Lord this coming year.

....

....

....

TUESDAY

DEEPENING YOUR DESIRE

As we begin this year, it seems appropriate to begin by ask-ing the Lord to deepen our desire for His joy. I don't know what has held your desire captive or what your priorities have been, but I do believe that God can deepen our desire and reorder our priorities.

Maybe you have made some new-year commitments about what you'd like to accomplish. If not, take a few minutes to list some here. If you already have that list, pull it out and rewrite it below. Across the top of your list write, "Above all these things, I choose joy."

Part time work - more money to pay off some of my debt

WEDNESDAY

DELIGHTING IN THE LORD

"*Delight yourself in the LORD*" (Psalm 37:4). To delight ourselves in the Lord means that we find our joy in the Lord. Delighting in the Lord means turning from worldliness toward godliness. Changing from building our own treasure on earth toward discovering that Jesus is the treasure to be esteemed on this earth.

Will you approach this year of choosing joy with delight? Maybe you have chosen this devotional because you desperately need the joy of the Lord. Maybe you are like a woman

has never experienced joy. Maybe you have
id long to be filled with it. Maybe you have
f the Christian life, but never the delight.

lutes to write what you need from the Lord:

joy, peace, direction
new belief, new relationship
in him

꧁꧂ **THURSDAY** ꧁꧂
FIGHTING FOR JOY

John Piper says that we must fight for joy. I agree with him
wholeheartedly. We must fight for the relationship that
God has called us to. We must fight against our very natures
to become the joy-filled people of God. We must fight our sin
and countless distractions. And for some, you will even have
to fight against the ones you love so that the pursuit of joy
becomes your priority.

"Rejoice in the Lord!" (Philippians 3:1). In this scripture,
God actually commands us to rejoice in Him. For many, learning to rejoice will mean that we will have to fight for joy.

Will you have to fight for joy? What are the already obvious opponents in your battle?

Relationship = non-believer

THE WEEKEND
RADICAL JOY

Choosing joy in your everyday life means more than just knowing the right things to think. The correct passages to quote. The theological doctrines of joy.

Choosing joy is a radical decision to honor God by experiencing the depths of God's promises to us. It's desiring Him above all else, rejoicing in His character, and living joyfully, according to His Word.

Radical joy is sin-destroying, world-changing, wound-healing, other-centered, and mission-minded. Radical joy creates a God-glorifying life. This year, may we choose radical, sold-out joy. Come alive joy. Passionate joy. Change-me-completely kind of joy.

This weekend, write a joy mission statement for yourself. What do you really want? And how do you propose to get there? When you're done, take a few minutes and dedicate that plan to the Lord.

....

....

....

For there exists a delight that is not given to the wicked, but to those honoring Thee, O God, without desiring recompense, the joy of whom Thou art Thyself! And this is the blessed life, to rejoice towards Thee, about Thee, for Thy sake.
—*Augustine*[1]

Always

MONDAY

JUST PLAIN "ALWAYS"

Be joyful always.
—I Thessalonians 5:16

My assignment was to write fifty-two weeks of devotionals about joy. Cinchy. Easy-breezy. What a joy! What an honor. Tell me what Bible teacher wouldn't want to spend a few months studying the scriptures about joy. Praying about joy. Writing about joy. This assignment was the jackpot of book writing and I was thrilled to be the writer.

So I sat down to start outlining the fifty-two weeks. My outlining usually begins by pouring out the ideas and thoughts stored in my heart until they begin to take shape as a direction. I sat at my computer like I had strapped myself into a rocket ship. Eager to get started, ready to launch and write as fast as my little heart could process. So I created a new document called "Ideas for Joy" and began.

A few ideas came so I wrote them down. And then there was nothing. A couple more lines, then nothing again. *Surely,*

I just need to bear down and triple focus, this has to be inside of me, I believed. So I furrowed my brow and searched my mind and my understanding for those nuggets of joy. Here is the truth my searching uncovered: I still have much to learn about the scriptural application of joy.

Sitting at my computer with very little written on my outline, my head asked my heart, *Why don't you know very much about joy?* The joy outline revealed that I know lots about joy when there is obvious joy present in my circumstances or in my heart. Yep, I know the happy, dancing kind of joy. But the verse that highlights my lack is this one: *"Be joyful always."*

Always? Always meaning always? In all things? No matter where I am? Or who I am with? Always? The Bible, and therefore the Lord, did not stutter. God said **always**. No conditions. No limits. No qualifiers. Just plain always.

This great big truth is where we must begin. The God of the universe, the God of our creation, and the Designer of our humanity has commanded all who follow His Son, Jesus, to be joyful always. I imagine that God assigned this topic to me, not because I have a treasure chest of knowledge to pour out, but because I am lacking and His desire is that I would live in full obedience to His instruction. I believe this writing has been given to me so that I would study and learn, but even more important, so that my life would be transformed.

We are going to spend the next fifty-one weeks together searching, learning, and applying this powerful, radical, spirit-altering call from God. I pray that we both will be eternally changed. I also pray that the weeks will be so much more than an accumulation of knowledge. The Apostle Paul wrote the words "Be joyful always" so that our lives would become an expression of joy.

And so, we begin with the goal before us. We will spend

this year learning about joy, so that our mind, body, and soul will be changed. The goal of this year is to become a living expression of joy.

May this great truth transform your life and mine.

As you search your own heart for what you already know about joy, what thoughts come to mind?

....

....

....

☙ TUESDAY ☙
THE YEAR AHEAD

The instruction to "be joyful always" wasn't just written to the Thessalonians. Paul gave a similar instruction to the Philippians: *"Rejoice in the Lord, always. I will say it again, rejoice!"* (Philippians 4:4).

Today, take a few minutes to think about the year ahead. What areas of your life would be radically transformed by learning to "rejoice in the Lord, always"? List a few of those below and then take a few minutes to pray, specifically committing each one of those areas to the Lord. In effect, handing over to God all the places you long for him to work in your life toward joy.

Relationships

Love

Painting (joy)

WEDNESDAY

BE TRANSFORMED

As I began to realize how very little I knew about joy, I started to pray, *Lord, show me what I have been missing. Change me.* Read this passage from Romans 12:2 and write your own prayer for this year's joy journey below: *"Do not conform any longer to the pattern of this world, but be transformed by the renewing of your mind."*

Lord, please help me to fund
more joy in you, my heart
& mind & renew - refresh -
- Joy -

THURSDAY

WHAT'S YOUR JOY QUOTIENT?

Always means "at all times, unfailingly, habitually, continuously, endlessly." This week's key passage instructs us to be joyful always. Does that seem overwhelming to you? Impossible? The Bible would not require of us what we can never become. Circle the words below that best describe your current joy quotient?

Never	Sometimes	Seldom
Constant	Off and on	Random
Up and down	Dependent on others	Inconsistent

Pray with me: *Oh great God, will you meet me right where I am and begin to change my heart? I long to be joyful always. Amen.*

THE WEEKEND
OUR SOURCE FOR HOPE

In another familiar passage of scripture, Jesus Himself made a promise to us: *"And surely I am with you always, to the very end of the age"* (Matthew 28:20)

If you and I are called to "be joyful always," what hope does this promise give to you? Who will be our source and our guide on this journey toward transforming joy?

The powerful presence of Jesus will be with us always. He will be our guide as we learn to live always in His joy.

Spend this weekend observing. In these next few days, pay attention to the moments or circumstances where you experience joy. Don't force anything or manipulate your thoughts. Just pay attention to where you are and what gives you tastes of joy. We have a beautiful journey ahead, but this weekend, take some time to notice where you are beginning. Then jot down a few of your discoveries:

....

....

....

Scripture has but one sense,
which is the literal sense.
—*William Tyndale*
(1494–1536)

WEEK 3

Defined

DEFINING JOY

You have made known to me the path of life; you will fill me with
joy in your presence, with eternal pleasures at your right hand.
—Psalm 16:11

I've spent half the morning reading great thinkers' definitions of joy. Take a few minutes to read the ones I've chosen below. Use your pen to circle or underline the phrases and
words that mean something to you today.

JOY—The inner attitude of rejoicing in one's salvation
regardless of outward circumstances.[1]

JOY—A quality or attitude of delight and happiness,
which is ultimately grounded in the work of God as
Father, Son and Holy Spirit. Among the many situations in which joy is experienced, Scripture recognizes
being accepted in the presence of God as supreme.[2]

JOY—State of delight and well-being that results from
knowing and serving God. A number of Greek and

Hebrew words are used to convey the ideas of joy and rejoicing. We have the same situation in English with such nearly synonymous words as *happiness, pleasure, delight, gladness, merriment, felicity,* and *enjoyment.* The words *joy* and *rejoice* are the words used most often to translate the Hebrew and Greek words into English. Joy is found more than 150 times in the Bible. If such words as *joyous* and *joyful* are included, the number comes to more than 200. The verb *rejoice* appears well over 200 times.

Joy is the fruit of a right relation with God. It is not something people can create by their own efforts. The Bible distinguishes joy from pleasure.[3]

JOY—Christians have grounds for joy in both their experience of salvation and their hope of what God will do in the future.[4]

JOY—Positive human condition that can be either feeling or action. The Bible uses "joy" in both senses.[5]

Before we move past defining joy, why don't you take a minute to write your own definition of joy. I'll help you start:

Joy is . . .

....

....

....

❧ TUESDAY ❧
DEFINING THE "ALWAYS" KIND OF JOY

Yesterday, the last definition of joy stated that joy is both a feeling and an action. Last week we learned that God calls us to "be joyful always." When Paul wrote those words, he was using the "action" definition of joy. Those words mean joy is an action we can engage in, choose, and learn to have—regardless of how we "feel."

Oh my, do you see how important this definition is to us as we begin this journey toward living in joy every day? We can choose **the action of joy** no matter what our circumstances, even no matter our feelings.

Have you tried to "feel" joy all the time and felt like a miserable failure? Me too.

To "rejoice" means "to find joy in." Take a few minutes to write out this verse a few times. Then commit it to memory: *"Rejoice in the Lord always, I will say it again: Rejoice!"* (Philippians 4:4).

....

....

....

❧ WEDNESDAY ❧
CHOOSING TO LIVE IN JOY

Joy is a feeling *and* an action. But learning to live in everyday joy means that we choose the action of joy regardless of how we feel. Some of us haven't had very much practice in choosing joy, but this is the year everything changes! I believe we can become people of action. People of joy.

This very moment, think of the one place you most desperately need joy. Bow your head and spend a moment listening to God. Ask Him, "How can I choose the *action* of joy no matter how I *feel*?" Make a note here about God's answer:

....

....

....

THURSDAY
THE POWER TO CHOOSE

Any action requires motion. All motion requires power. The power to choose the action of joy will come to you by way of Jesus, through the Holy Spirit. The Holy Spirit fills the soul of every person who follows Jesus Christ. The Holy Spirit is the source of all spiritual power. The good news is that you don't have to be powerful enough or smart enough to begin the journey toward joy. It's the Holy Spirit who will give you what you need.

Many days, I declare to God, *I have nothing. You will have to be my all.* Maybe you feel the same way. In 1 Corinthians, Paul wants us to understand where his power comes from: *"My message and my preaching were not with wise and persuasive words, but with a demonstration of the Spirit's power, so that your faith might not rest on men's wisdom, but on God's power."* (1 Corinthians 2:4–5). In the very same way that Paul acquired wisdom, we too will acquire joy . . . God's power.

Take a minute to write a prayer, asking God to release the power of the Spirit in you and give you the ability to be *joyful*!

....

....

....

◈◈◈ THE WEEKEND ◈◈◈
A NEW DEFINITION

Why don't you take a poll this weekend? Ask your children. Ask your spouse. Your neighbor. Your pastor. Find out how the people in your life define this beautiful characteristic called joy.

Based on our time this week, why don't you write a new definition of the everyday joy that becomes your personal goal? This is the definition that I want you to begin praying for, asking God to transform your heart and give you this kind of joy.

....

....

....

◈ The very nature of joy makes nonsense of our common distinction between having and wanting. ◈
—*C. S. Lewis,* Surprised by Joy

WEEK 4

What *Has* Happened?

◦◦◦◦◦◦ **MONDAY** ◦◦◦◦◦◦
A POWERFUL LITTLE QUESTION

What has happened to all your joy?
—Galatians 4:15

When I was reading through the book of Galatians a few months ago, this verse stopped me right in my tracks. My head kept trying to read the next words, but Paul's question to the church was so powerful and relevant, I felt like he had jumped off the page and yelled at me. Me, for heaven's sake; he was yelling at *me*. Then he wouldn't leave me alone. For weeks, I kept hearing this question shout to me in the glorious and in the mundane. On airplanes, in my laundry room, laying on my pillow just moments away from sleep . . . *What has happened to all your joy?*

Now that I've had plenty of time to think about it, I'll tell you what's happened to mine. I had forgotten about joy. I had been so busy doing and becoming and scurrying that I hadn't given one intentional thought to the pursuit or the presence of joy. Embarrassing. Bible teachers ought to think about joy more often.

Honestly, I couldn't remember the last time I asked God to fill me with joy. Or to create a joyful spirit in my children. Goodness knows I've asked for peace and sanity and obedience. I've prayed for healing and wisdom. I've worshiped the Lord and studied His Word. But joy? How in the world did I forget about the beautiful, good, and pleasing gift of joy?

After months of yelling from this passage, God has my complete attention. *I want His joy!* To pursue His joy. To be filled with joy. To respond and react in joy. To discover new joy in my regular, old life. To give joy and multiply joy in the lives of my children. To teach about joy. To serve with greater joy. To love from the deep well of joy.

What scares me is that my life is flying by. Without that Galatians shout-out, I could have spent the next who knows how many years living morally, loving and serving, but possibly missing the fullness of joy that God desires for me.

Do you know how grateful I am that God has divinely given me the assignment of learning more about joy? Eternally grateful. Do you know how much I want you to hear that same verse calling your soul awake? So very much.

Paul remembered the joy of the Galatians when they first came to Christ. But since he had been with them, other men had come in, given new instructions, and stolen their hearts. When Paul wrote to the Galatians in chapter 4, he was specifically rebuking them for leaning into the laws that caused them to lose their joy. They had forgotten about joy.

Maybe this verse is shouting to you today in much the same way it shouted to me . . . *What has happened to all your joy?*

As we begin this week together, how would you answer that question?

....

....

....

TUESDAY
DISTRACTED FROM JOY

The church in Galatia had become distracted by trying to keep all the laws. They sacrificed their joy on the altar of rule-keeping. Even smaller things have distracted me. Things like buying birthday cards and trying to get those things in the mail, making some kind of dinner every night, and potty training the puppies. Actually, I have let almost everything become a distraction, when in fact, God has called me to keep my eyes on the source of my joy—Him.

Quick, name the first five things that easily distract you from joy:

1. ....

2. ....

3. ....

4. ....

5. ....

WEDNESDAY

TURNING AWAY FROM DISTRACTION

Everyone I know longs to live in the fullness of joy, yet I can count on one hand the people I'm close to who truly live that way. I don't believe the choice to live without joy is intentional. Maybe we have just become accustomed to living without joy, so we have lost the deep craving.

Let's pray this prayer together, *God, please show me what has happened to my joy.*

And now this prayer, *God, I repent . . .*

....

....

....

THURSDAY

"DO YOU WANT IT?"

"*Jesus went up to Jerusalem for a feast of the Jews. Now there is in Jerusalem near the Sheep Gate a pool, which in Aramaic is called Bethesda and which is surrounded by five colonnades. Here a great number of disabled people used to lie—the blind, the lame, the paralyzed. One who was there had been an invalid for thirty-eight years. When Jesus saw him lying there and learned that he had been in this condition for a long time, he asked him, 'Do you want to get well?'* " (John 5:1–6).

Our condition is not always accompanied by a conscious awareness of what we need. Sometimes we grow so familiar with our condition that we become desensitized to what we could become.

Jesus wanted to know if this sick man had the desire to get well. In just the same way, I have heard Him ask of me, "Do you want to live in my joy?" If my response is sincerely "Yes," then Jesus is my answer.

So, my friend, do you want to live in the joy of the Lord? What has desensitized you to who you can become?

....

....

....

 THE WEEKEND

WILLING TO CHANGE

Do you want to live every day filled with the joy of the Lord? Do you long for eyes to see joy, even when circumstances are difficult or the path is unclear? Do you want more than an inconsistent feeling that rises and falls with each new e-mail? If so, hear Jesus' words to the man by the pool: " *'Get up! Pick up your mat and walk'* " (John 5:8).

With all my heart, I believe that Jesus can spiritually fill us with His joy and radically transform our lives. Our countenances. Our attitudes. Our actions.

This weekend, will you begin a prayer walk with me? As you walk through your house, through your day, through your schedule, begin praying for these things:

- *Wisdom to understand* your lack of joy and your need for joy.

- *A willingness to change.* The man at the pool had laid there for thirty-eight years. It felt normal to him. Ask God to show you what feels normal for you but is really unhealthy.
- *Obedience to pursue joy.* If Jesus tells you to pick up your mat and walk, will you?

Record here what you discovered through your prayers:

....

....

....

❧ We can do nothing well without joy. ❧
—Sibbes

WEEK 5

Restored

*Restore to me the **joy** of your salvation,*
and uphold me with a willing spirit.
—Psalm 51:12, ESV

To him who is able to keep you from stumbling and to present you
*blameless before the presence of his glory with great **joy**, to the only*
God, our Savior, through Jesus Christ our Lord, be glory, majesty,
dominion, and authority, before all time and now and forever. Amen.
—Jude 24–25, ESV

Stolen joy. There must be an epidemic. Everywhere I go people are suffering from lack of joy. Maybe they had joy in their possession, if only for a moment, but then it was gone. Almost everyone I know has been robbed of joy, in one way or another. I believe it's time for the people of God to have their joy restored.

There have been seasons in my life when setback after setback piled on top of me. Broken relationships. Failed plans.

Really difficult finances. Heartaches over my children. My joy was stolen, and my soul went dark.

Have you ever read your Bible and prayed, but the words didn't seem to resonate? You asked several friends for wise counsel, they said the right things, you felt your head nodding in agreement, but your soul remained empty? Have you ever gone through the motions of searching for joy, but nothing powerful stirred inside of you? You've had your joy stolen, too. In Psalm 51, David grieved over the sin that had stolen his joy. Maybe you lost your joy another way. A long season of difficulties, frustration with your physical body, weariness from your never-ending responsibilities. No matter what has taken your joy, I want to encourage you to join me in praying David's prayer, *"Oh sweet Lord, restore to me the joy of your salvation."*

This week is about joy restoration. I want you to take a deep breath and relax. You don't have the strategy or the power to do this on your own. You couldn't even if you wanted to. It's God's work. We are going to ask the Lord for His restoration.

We have begun in prayer, but take a minute to think back. When was the last time you remember experiencing joy?

....

....

....

⦿⦿⦿ TUESDAY ⦿⦿⦿
WE SERVE A JOYFUL GOD!

Some people think of God as a killjoy, as if He's trying to take all the fun out of everything. But nothing could be further from the truth. *"May the glory of the LORD endure forever; may the LORD rejoice in his works"* (Psalm 104:31). God Himself knows joy, and He wants us to pursue joy. So it's incredibly appropriate that we turn our prayers toward God to ask for joy restored.

This world may steal your joy, but that does not come from God. He desires that we live restored. Full. Passionate. Victorious. Look up Isaiah 65:18 and write it below to remind you today of God's desires for his people.

....

....

....

⦿⦿⦿ WEDNESDAY ⦿⦿⦿
"RENEW A STEADFAST SPIRIT IN ME"

"Create in me a pure heart, O God, and renew a steadfast spirit within me" (Psalm 51:10). In his prayer of restoration, David asks God for a pure heart and a steadfast spirit. David comes with his great need and asks God to be the creator and renewer.

Let's ask God to be both of those today. Fill in the blanks of the prayer below:

God, I come to you for my joy restored. Will you come and create ....*? Will you renew*................................*?*

I place all my needs in your hands. Lord, will you restore what has been stolen? I long to live in your joy. Amen.

THURSDAY
SHARE YOUR STORY OF JOY

Do you remember when you first understood that your sins have been forgiven? That Jesus died for you? Your name is written in the book of life. Heaven and eternity are yours. Do you remember the joy of coming into relationship with the God of creation? That is the joy David is praying for in Psalm 51:12 when he says, *"Restore to me the joy of your salvation."*

He is asking for a fresh remembrance. A fresh humbling over the great gift that has been given. A new awe.

Maybe one of the sweetest ways that I am able to recall the joy of my salvation is by telling someone else what God has done for me.

Need joy restoration? It may begin to return when you tell someone else how God saved you. Make a few notes in preparation.

....

....

....

THE WEEKEND
FIGHT FOR JOY

"The thief comes only to steal and kill and destroy; I have come that they may have life, and have it to the full" (John 10:10).

We all know who has stolen your joy. The thief called Satan. It's just that he can't keep it. God has bigger plans for you and for me. God sent His Son, Jesus, so that we could live abundant, full lives. So I beg you, fight for joy. Keep choosing joy.

Maybe you have lived discouraged and joyless for so long now, your joy is gone and hope went with it. I plead with you, don't give up. You see, I believe God. I believe He's really big and completely able to restore your joy. I have never met a person too far gone from God. I believe His Word, and based on His promises, He's coming.

So, until God fully restores your joy, feelings and all, would you still keep choosing joy as an act of your obedience?

May we choose joy on this earth to lift high the name of our Savior, Jesus. May the God of joy be glorified in our choosing. May His work be done through us as we choose joy from day to day. May you be blessed beyond measure because you have humbled your heart and chosen to live every second on this earth *with joy*.

Write about your journey of joy this year. Give thanks for the things God has done and will do.

....

....

....

He prays to God and finds favor with him, he sees God's face and shouts for joy; he is restored by God to his righteous state.

—Job 33:26

WEEK 6

Given by God

For to the one who pleases him
God has given wisdom and knowledge and joy.
—Ecclesiastes 2:26 ESV

You have filled my heart with greater joy than when
their grain and new wine abound.
—Psalm 4:7

This past week I had the great privilege of meeting with several wives of PGA golfers for Bible study and prayer. Later that night, my husband and I were invited to the golfers' fellowship for dinner, study, worship, and prayer. As this wonderful day drew to a close, the chaplain of the PGA, Larry Moody, spent a few minutes telling Scott and me beautiful stories of God's work in this ministry.

One of the most powerful stories he told us was about a golfer who several years ago had won most of the major tournaments. He was the talk of the sportscasters and golfing fans.

That year, on an almost unbeatable streak, he played in Augusta and won the prestigious green jacket at The Masters.

The next morning, his picture was on the front page of all the newspapers delivered to his room. The *New York Times*. The *Atlanta Constitution*. His face was on every broadcast with play-by-play commentary of his brilliant plays. As Larry tells the story, this great golfer turned to his wife that morning and said, "They lied to me."

"What do you mean?" she responded.

"Here I am making the most money anyone has ever made in the sport of golf. I have won all these majors, and yesterday was the biggest win of my life. I am married to a beautiful woman. I travel in private jets all over this world. The news media loves me. But they lied to me. People told me if I could just get to this place in life, it would be enough. They lied. Something is missing. I have accomplishment. I do not have joy."

Only three days later, that accomplished golfer was invited to attend the Bible study Larry Moody has faithfully taught at the PGA for more than thirty years. The man didn't even know what a Bible study was, but for some reason, he accepted an invitation to go. Larry says that he was teaching through the book of John and that night the verse of study was John 3:16: *"For God so loved the world that he gave his one and only Son, that whoever believes in him shall not perish but have eternal life."*

For the first time in his life, the world-famous golfer heard that a relationship with Jesus Christ is what makes us whole. Accomplishments in this world are to be enjoyed, but they cannot give us joy. The true gift of joy comes to us from Jesus. A few days after he'd accomplished everything he could dream of and still found himself empty, the golfer asked Jesus Christ to be His Savior. For the first time in his life, he finally understood what it means to be filled by the joy of the Lord.

Since God is the author of all creation, He is also the source of all joy. Any real joy that we have on this earth comes to us as a gift from God. He is the one who fills our hearts with joy and even greater joy.

In my own life, I have already spent too many years living like that golfer had. Looking for joy in accomplishments, things, and wealth. Maybe you have done the same thing too. As we begin this week together, let's take a minute to write a couple of definitions. What is the difference between these two?

1. Enjoying the things we have been given.

2. Receiving the gift of joy from God, who is the giver.

....

....

....

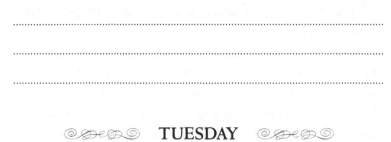

TUESDAY
GOD GIVES JOY

Read this passage with me: *"Every good and perfect gift is from above, coming down from the Father of the heavenly lights, who does not change like shifting shadows"* (James 1:17).

God is the giver of joy, and God is the giver of good and perfect gifts. If you and I are going to live in an everyday joy, we will have to remember that true joy comes from God—from the filling of His spirit, from the goodness of His gifts.

Have you pursued the "good and perfect gift" of joy that God generously extends to each of us—to you? Make a list of some of the gifts God has given you. Is joy on your list? If it's not, take a minute to write out a prayer asking God to open your eyes and heart to His gift of joy:

....

....

....

WEDNESDAY
CELEBRATING GOD'S GOODNESS OVER JOY

Read the following verse—out loud: *"They will celebrate your abundant goodness and joyfully sing of your righteousness"* (Psalm 145:7).

Every joy we will experience on this earth is the product of God's goodness to us. He is the giver! When our lives celebrate the goodness of God, we are filled with joy.

Today, no matter what you are facing, how can you celebrate the goodness of God? Where do you see His abundant goodness in your life?

....

....

....

THURSDAY
A SONG OF CELEBRATION

Go back to the verse at the beginning of yesterday's reading, Psalm 145:7. In our culture and in the place where you live, what would it mean to *"joyfully sing of [God's] righteousness"*? An actual song? The joyful countenance of your face? The compassion of your words?

Sometimes we forget to joyfully sing with our lives. Has God been good to you, and you have forgotten to sing and celebrate? What about spending the next few moments praying a prayer of celebration back to God. Write that prayer here:

THE WEEKEND
CELEBRATING THE GIVER

God is the giver of joy. Oh hallelujah! We cannot manufacture our joy or buy our joy or accomplish our joy. True and abiding joy will always come from God. This weekend, let's celebrate the giver of joy! I'm thinking this weekend would be a great time to choose one person or one cause and bombard that selection with a celebration of your joy.

Bombard means "to continuously attack." Persistently. What if you bombard with giving? Maybe you choose a neighbor or a friend and just flat-out shock them with an outpouring of kindness and joy. Or maybe you decide to bombard a ministry with your time.

However you decide to celebrate, I pray these next few days, this one truth sinks deep into your soul: God is the giver of my joy.

Take a minute to write out your plan:

....

....

....

When it is all said and done, only God can create joy in God. This is why the old saints not only pursued joy but prayed for it.

—John Piper[1]

JOY

Was Born

But the angel said to them, "Do not be afraid.
I bring you good news of great joy that will be for all the people.
Today in the town of David a Savior has been born to you;
he is Christ the Lord."
—Luke 2:10–11

Over two thousand years ago an angel appeared to shepherds while they were tending their flocks of sheep. I have no idea what the shepherds' lives were like before the angel, but I do know that the news he delivered changed everything. For all of us. For all eternity.

In this one announcement, God brushed aside the fears of mankind and provided the world with the reason for joy. Joy had been born. Our Savior had come. He came for the shepherds, and He came for you and me. We call the angel's news the gospel, which means the revelation of Christ. And because the gospel is good news of great joy, we do not have to be afraid.

Joy was born in a stable. Divinely appointed. Sweetly introduced to this world through the humble, ordinary birth of a baby. Joy came to this earth as a gift from God. A baby born to become the Savior. Born to save the world. Born so that we might have joy. Great, great joy.

As we begin this year of looking for joy, we must begin with this foundational truth: deep and abiding joy will come to us only through a relationship with Jesus. Jesus is the reason for joy. He is the source and the fullness of joy. We are introduced to real joy when we ask Jesus to be our Savior.

Maybe you've spent half a lifetime looking for joy in hundreds of different places. I have certainly had my fair share of dead-end joy pursuits. But joy cannot be bought or manipulated or earned. Joy does not come to us through possessions or accomplishment. Somebody besides Jesus cannot give us a lasting joy. The kind of joy I desire, the kind of joy our soul longs for, was born as a baby named Jesus.

Sometimes I pray, *Oh God, help me know the gospel more and more every day. I want to understand it. I want to be able to give a clear presentation of who you are to everyone I meet. Teach me how to live the joy of the gospel even more powerfully today. Amen.*

If the gospel is the good news of great joy, then take a few minutes today to think it through. We'll spend this week building our understanding of the gospel, but for now, you can write your own definition below:

The gospel is . . .

....

....

....

❦❦❧ TUESDAY ❦❦❧
A MESSAGE OF JOY

In the Greek language, the word *gospel* means "good news" or a "message bringing joy." That is exactly what the birth of Jesus was, good news. A message intended to bring joy for all people.

Too many times, the message of Jesus has not been communicated clearly. The gospel of Jesus has many times been told as a message of condemnation or separation. But the intent of the New Testament is that the life and message of Jesus be communicated as a message of joy.

Write your name in the following blank: *"But the angel said to _____, 'Do not be afraid. I bring you good news of great joy that will be for all the people. Today in the town of David a Savior has been born to you; he is Christ the Lord' "* (Luke 2:10–11).

Now answer the following:

What is the good news?
....

Who is the good news for?
....

How are we supposed to respond to the good news?
....

WEDNESDAY
JOY THROUGH JESUS

I don't know about you, but I find it comforting to understand that joy comes through Jesus. I do not have to figure this out. I can't produce joy or build a bigger, better version of joy. Joy, in its fullness, was made alive in Christ. I can live in joy because of Jesus. My life hidden in Him can be filled by the joy He brought to this earth. What a relief to know that I don't have to create joy; I only have to join my Savior in the joy He brought to earth.

In prayer, why don't you spend some time with God turning away from your efforts to find joy apart from Him.

Then think about this: have you tried to manufacture your own joy? Take a few minutes to jot down a few of your attempts to make your own joy:

....

....

....

THURSDAY
THERE IS NO FEAR IN JOY

"*Do not be afraid.*" Every time God says that in the Bible, my spirit takes a deep breath. The angel announced the birth of joy with this instruction: Do not be afraid.

Do you feel afraid today? Then let your heart remember the good news of great joy. We have a Savior. We can put our life into His faithful hands and then trust. We can be forgiven of our sins. We live today on this earth, trusting that heaven is our home.

The message of the gospel is the message of being saved. Saved from the penalty of sin. Saved from living a purposeless life. Saved from being lost for all eternity. Saved from a life of fear. Read these tender words of Jesus: *"Peace I leave with you; my peace I give you. I do not give to you as the world gives. Do not let your heart be troubled and do not be afraid"* (John 14:27).

To have a relationship with The Reason for Joy means that we can have peace instead of trouble or fear. What will you choose today?

....

....

....

THE WEEKEND
GOOD NEWS IN THE DARK NIGHT

That night in their fields, the shepherds were enduring yet another dark night, until a glorious messenger from heaven came with great news of joy. Maybe you feel like you are enduring yet another dark season, another difficult week, another gloomy day. I want you to know that the message the angel gave all those years ago is the message God has for you. There is good news of great joy, my friend. You do not have to be afraid.

This weekend, spend some time with your heart before God. Bring him what is dark and gloomy. Bring him your fears. Every one of us will endure dark seasons in our lives, but if we are looking for good news, we must remember the gospel. What good news can you see in your dark night?

....

....

....

Earth's joy is small, her mirth is trivial, but heaven has sent us joy immeasurable, fit for immortal minds.
                              —*Charles Haddon Spurgeon*

Is the Good News
of Salvation

DO YOU BELIEVE?

I delight greatly in the LORD;
*my soul **rejoices** in my God.*
For he has clothed me with garments of salvation
and arrayed me in a robe of righteousness,
as a bridegroom adorns his head like a priest,
and as a bride adorns herself with her jewels.
—Isaiah 61:10

Almost every weekend I have the great privilege of sharing the good news about Jesus with women of every age.
I will never, ever tire of watching grown-up women make the
decision to follow Christ with their lives. It always feels like a
miracle to me.

We are stubborn people, and most of us do not like to
change. Many of us would rather continue with our familiar
lives, even if the burden of sin is overwhelming. That's why

it takes my breath away to watch a grown woman ask Jesus to be her Savior. I love to watch all the lights come on, as the mind and heart finally understand who Jesus is and how much He loves her. I love to see her receive forgiveness instead of condemnation. To choose hope instead of despair. To watch a woman lay down the heavy load of defeat and choose a new life with Jesus makes the soul rejoice.

The good news about salvation is this:

- God who is holy made us in His image to know Him.
- But we sinned and cut ourselves off from God.
- In His great love, God sent His Son, Jesus, to live a perfect life, die on the cross, and take the punishment for the sins of all who would believe in Him.
- Jesus rose on the third day, defeating death.
- Jesus now calls us to turn away from our sin and trust in Him alone for our forgiveness, so that we might be saved from the penalty of sin, which is eternal death.
- He calls us to become His followers. To have a relationship with Him.
- When we believe that Jesus is our Savior, we are promised a new life with God here on earth and for all eternity in heaven.

Isaiah said he delights greatly in the Lord, who clothed him with garments of salvation and a robe of righteousness. Salvation is a free gift from God for any who would believe. And salvation is a reason for great, great joy! For rejoicing and dancing and bell-ringing! To be free of the burden of sin, to be forgiven by a holy God, oh hallelujah! To watch someone step from bondage into freedom is the most beautiful sight I've ever seen. The soul rejoices when the burden is gone.

For several weeks, we've been building this teaching, one Scripture truth on top of the other coming to this foundational understanding: you and I will never know joy apart from a relationship with God through His Son, Jesus.

Today the question is, *Do you believe the good news of Jesus?*

Search your heart and share it here:

....

....

....

༼ TUESDAY ༽
GOOD NEWS FOR THE SINNER

D o you remember the angel's announcement from last week's study: *"I bring you good news of great joy that will be for all the people"*? Now read these passages:

"For all have sinned and fall short of the glory of God" (Romans 3:23).

"For the wages of sin is death, but the gift of God is eternal life in Christ Jesus our Lord" (Romans 6:23).

Answer the following:

Who has sinned?

....

What is the consequence of sin?

....

What is the gift of God?

....

⊙⊱✎⊰⊙ WEDNESDAY ⊙⊱✎⊰⊙
DECIDING TO FOLLOW JESUS

Perhaps today you want to settle your relationship with God once and for all. If you want your sins to be forgiven and to become a follower of Christ, just pray this prayer to God. He has been waiting all this time. . . .

God, I believe that Jesus is your Son. I believe He died to pay the penalty for my sins. Please forgive me of my sins. Make me a member of the family of God on this earth and for all eternity. Teach me how to follow you and live for your glory. Amen.

"The jailer brought them into his house and set a meal before them; he was filled with joy because he had come to believe in God—he and his whole family" (Acts 16:34).

In the verse above, what was it that produced joy in the jailer? How can you allow that same source to fill you with joy?

....

....

....

THURSDAY
RECEIVED BY GOD

I want you to understand something: God does not make the gift of salvation complicated. People have done that. God does not move the target or make the good news too difficult to understand. He is not wishy-washy. He does not play games with us.

When I was growing up, I never really had an assurance that I had followed Christ correctly, so I probably asked Jesus to be my Savior hundreds of times. As an adult, seeking God for wisdom, I finally heard in my spirit . . . *Angela, I had you the first time.* God does not try to trick us. He knows our hearts.

Read these words from Jesus and speak your own prayers of thanksgiving: *"My sheep listen to my voice; I know them, and they follow me. I give them eternal life, and they shall never perish; no one can snatch them out of my hand"* (John 10:27–28).

Can you imagine my great joy and relief when I finally understood the heart of God? If you believe in Him, He receives you into the family of God. Sins forgiven. Eternal life secure. Amen.

What do you believe about the heart of God? Share your experience with His forgiveness.

....

....

....

THE WEEKEND
THE REJOICING OF ANGELS

"*In the same way, I tell you, there is rejoicing in the presence of the angels of God over one sinner who repents*" (Luke 15:10).

The forgiven want to give what they have been given. This weekend, ask God for wisdom to know who needs to hear the good news of great joy. Maybe you could clearly explain the good news of Jesus to one of your children. Maybe God will direct you to a friend or to a stranger. Either way, this gift of great joy is to be shared.

May the rejoicing of angels be multiplied as we lead others to the joy we have received.

Write a prayer for wisdom and direction regarding who you might share God's good news with; then write the name of whoever God puts on your heart:

....

....

....

The French philosopher Voltaire was an unbeliever of the worst kind, attacking the Christian faith in his prolific writing. But on his deathbed he said: "I wish I had never been born." And his death was so frightening that the nurse who looked after him said, "For all the wealth of Europe I would never want to see another unbeliever die. Joy is not found in unbelief."

JOY
Is a Fruit of the Spirit

*But the fruit of the Spirit is love, **joy**, peace, patience,
kindness, goodness, faithfulness, gentleness and self-control.*
—Galatians 5:22–23

At the beginning of this past year, I began to pray this verse for my life differently than I ever have before. The Bible teaches that the Holy Spirit comes to live inside of us when we ask Jesus to be our Savior. And it is the Holy Spirit living inside of us that produces the very fruit I desire for my life. Several months ago I began to pray, "Holy Spirit, fill me with all of your fruit! I want everything you have to give. Every gift. Every part of this verse. Not just a taste, but the whole thing."

I truly long to be filled to the measure of all fullness with the alive, powerful presence of the Holy Spirit. And I desire all that He wants to bring . . . love, joy, peace, patience, kindness, goodness, faithfulness, and self-control. I am learning that this fruit will not come to me because I am trying harder at being joyful or patient or any of the rest. I will become a joyful person because the Holy Spirit has been set free inside of me to produce abundant fruit in my life.

But what moves the Holy Spirit? Read Jesus' words in John 15:5: *"I am the vine, you are the branches. If a man remains in me and I in him, he will bear much fruit, apart from me you can do nothing."*

Do you see the key word? The action word in this verse is *remains*. This is the key to Holy Spirit fruit in our lives. Remaining with God. Abiding. Staying with Him. Following Him. Running hard after Him. In this same John 15 passage, Jesus gives a progression. He says:

> *If we stay with God* . . . . *we bear* spiritual *fruit.*
> *If we keep on staying* . . . . *we bear* more *fruit.*
> *If we keep on, keep on* . . . . *we bear* much *fruit.*

Staying with Jesus brings a progression of spiritual maturity whereby our lives bear the fruit of the Holy Spirit. That's what I want!

So if we are going to become women who are filled with the joy of the Holy Spirit, and all the other fruit, we must remain faithful, passionate followers of Jesus.

According to Galatians 5:23, where does our joy come from?

And according to John 15 (read verses 1–11 if you have time), how is spiritual fruit produced in our lives?

....

....

....

TUESDAY
LIVE WHAT YOU BELIEVE

I hope you are beginning to see that there is a beautiful relationship between spiritual fruit and the presence of the Holy Spirit. We cannot buy joy at the store or manufacture it with our minds. We will become full of joy because we allow the Holy Spirit to work powerfully in our lives.

The first step toward a life of joy is to become a follower of Jesus Christ. The second step is to stay with Jesus, growing and learning what it means to be a Christian. Finally, you and I will produce the fruit of joy in our lives as we choose to live what we believe.

Have you ever considered what it means to "live what you believe"? Is there an area of your life where you are not intentionally living what you believe? Maybe you believe the Bible is God's truth for our lives but haven't chosen to study it deeply. Maybe you believe in the power of prayer but haven't yet become a person of consistent prayer.

Take some time today to consider where you might begin really living what you believe. Jot down some notes to yourself here:

....

....

....

WEDNESDAY
REMAINING WITH JESUS

The Holy Spirit produces the fruit of joy in our lives because we choose to remain with Jesus. The word *remain* can also be translated *abide*, meaning to "follow, to stick to, to obey." The Bible is so clear. The power that God offers to each one of us through the Holy Spirit comes to us when we abide.

How consistent is your abiding with Jesus?

Do you long to know Him more? Regularly spend time with Him? Just so you know, God longs for you and He does not scold you when you return to Him. His love is not fickle, so He does not withhold Himself from any who seek Him.

What would it mean to rearrange your life around the commitment to abide with Jesus?

....

....

....

THURSDAY
THE FULLNESS OF JOY

If keeping a relationship with Jesus is the source of all power and spiritual fruit in our lives, I can't think of anything more important for each of us. The work of the Holy Spirit inside of us grows as we are faithful to keep our relationship with Jesus vital and thriving.

If I pray that I want all the Holy Spirit can give to me, my responsibility is to give my whole heart, mind, and soul to my relationship with Jesus. *"We have not received the spirit of the world but the Spirit who is from God, that we may understand what God has freely given us"* (1 Corinthians 2:12).

God has freely given us joy, JOY! And the fullness of joy will come from the Holy Spirit as I continue in relationship with Jesus.

Joy.

More joy.

Much joy.

How is it that someone who has few worldly possessions or little accomplishment on earth can be filled to the fullness with joy?

How then will you and I pursue the fullness of joy?

....

....

....

THE WEEKEND
LEARNING TO ABIDE WITH JESUS

Let this weekend be the beginning of a more consistent relationship with Jesus. In these days, consider how you might schedule your commitment to a faithful relationship with Him.

Here are some ideas to get you thinking:

- Find a daily Bible study to guide your time with Jesus.
- Ask your spouse to pray with you or read the Bible with you daily.

- Sign up for a daily online devotional that is sent directly to your e-mail.
- Shop around and buy a Bible that you really enjoy holding and reading.

Let me pray for you and me:

Oh Jesus, we want to faithfully abide with you. Learn more about you. Grow in spiritual maturity. By the power of the Holy Spirit, would you make us stronger, godly, and wise. Amen.

❧ *It is okay to possess more joy than people around you. It is one of the greatest gifts we can give. They need our joy.* ❧

—*Unknown*

WEEK 10

Comes from Understanding God's Word

MONDAY
UNDERSTANDING BRINGS JOY

When your words came, I ate them;
*they were my **joy** and my heart's delight,*
for I bear your name, O LORD God Almighty.
—Jeremiah 15:16

"I am coming to you now,
but I say these things while I am still in the world,
*so that they may have the full measure of my **joy** within them."*
—John 17:13

Right out of college, I moved back home and began working with the students at my church in North Carolina. Those junior and senior high kids became the loud megaphone God used to shout my call into ministry. I loved those kids. I

loved being part of their lives—praying for them, planning re-
treats for them. But the thing I loved most was watching them
begin to understand the Word of God.

There were two things that happened when the light of
understanding turned on in a student. First, there was the
"aha," where a new truth about God began to make sense. You
could feel the joy that came to them as the light turned on. It
was a contagious kind of joy that swept through the room as
student after student understood.

Second, there was the beauty of watching students imple-
ment truth in their lives. Nothing has ever moved me like seeing the Word of God come alive in a person. Watching those
students change their lives because they understood the Bible quickly became the foundation of my purpose in life. God
used those kids to call me to teach His Word, so that others
may know Him more.

In the book of Nehemiah, chapter 8, when the words of
God were first declared to the people, they wept. They wept
because they saw themselves as guilty before God. But when
they had understanding, they rejoiced. They rejoiced because
they understood the promises made to those who repent and
change. And because the people came to understand the words
of God, they had hope.

Do you know the Word of God? Do you understand the
promises He has made to you? Pray with me as we begin this
week together:

*God, I want to know Your Word. I desire understanding. I long
for the joy that comes from believing Your promises to me. I want to
celebrate the hope I have in You. Lord, teach me Your Word. Make it
sweet and fresh to me. Give me a new thirst to know You more.
Amen.*

Read Nehemiah 8:1–12. What thoughts and feelings does this reading stir in your heart?

....

....

....

⟨⟨⟨ **TUESDAY** ⟩⟩⟩
TASTE THE WORD OF GOD

If understanding the Word of God brings joy, then today, my friend, what decision will you make? To stay where you are with God or to seek to understand Him more?

Life can be so crazy busy for most of us that spending the time to understand God's Word seems out of reach. *Maybe later, when I'm retired and have more time. Maybe after the kids are grown.* We each have our own legitimate reasons not to add anything new to our already overscheduled lives.

The reason this devotional is broken into tiny, short bites of Bible teaching is for this very reason. We may not have much time, but we can take a little taste of God's Word every day. I'm praying for you as I write, that as we look for joy every day, these little tastes will only make you want the Word of God more. What are you hungry for that God's Word might supply?

....

....

....

WEDNESDAY
NOURISHMENT FOR THE SOUL

The prophet Jeremiah said, *"When your words came, I ate them; they were my joy and my heart's delight"* (Jeremiah 15:16).

What did Jeremiah do with the words of God?

How can you translate that phrase and apply it to your everyday life?

Notice that the joy came after the words had been taken in. You and I can sit in church and hear the Word. We can look at our copy of the Bible and read the Word. But the joy comes in receiving the Word of God like it is nourishment for our souls.

Understanding God's Word feeds our souls. And the well-fed soul is full of joy.

What words of God have you eaten that have given you great delight?

....

....

....

THURSDAY
HUNGRY FOR UNDERSTANDING

One of the phrases that radically changed my life was this line from a song: "I have decided to live what I believe."

To believe and to live are radically different things. If you believe that understanding the Word of God gives joy (and here we are spending a year looking for joy), then it seems like the logical next step is that we purpose to increase our understanding.

Maybe that means you begin to study the Bible for the very first time. Maybe it means that you go a little deeper or take steps to apply Bible truth to your life. Too many people live in fear of God's Word because they do not understand it. We want the joy of understanding! We want new lights to be turned on!

What darkness in your life would you like God's Word to dispel with His light?

....

....

....

THE WEEKEND
HUNGRY TO LEARN

One of the first ways to understand the Word of God more is to study under a teacher who has greater understanding than we do. After I had been working with the students in my hometown for a year, I knew it was time to go to seminary. My understanding had run out. I had given them everything I knew. I needed more to give to this purpose that God had called me to.

These days, I have the great privilege of studying the Word of God as a profession, and I continue to seek teachers further along in understanding so that I can learn from them.

At the church I attend, the pastor is a great Bible teacher. Every Sunday morning, I learn from him. New truths. New applications. New understanding. This weekend take an inventory of your Bible teachers. Do they faithfully teach from the Bible? Do they give you greater understanding?

If the answer is no, maybe this is the weekend to begin finding the people who will teach you more of the Word of God.

Who in your life could teach you more of God's Word? What can you do to move closer to that person so you can learn?

....

....

....

✎ *I call the New Testament the Book of Joy.*
There is nowhere in the world another book that is
pervaded with such a spirit of exhilaration. ✏
—*Henry Ward Beecher,* Archives

Is Promised to Christ Followers

REMEMBERING OUR SALVATION

I will clothe her priests with salvation,
and her saints will ever sing for joy.
—Psalm 132:16

And the ransomed of the LORD will return.
They will enter Zion with singing;
everlasting joy will crown their heads.
Gladness and joy will overtake them,
and sorrow and sighing will flee away.
—Isaiah 35:10

When we put our faith in God, we are saying to Him, I believe in who you are. I believe that the Bible is your Word. I believe you keep your promises.

The passage in Psalm 132 recounts a collection of promises God has made to His people. In the middle of that collection, God promised there would be joy for His saints. *Saint* doesn't mean perfect one, it means "one set apart for God." That's you and me and all who follow Him.

The followers of God are promised that we will "ever sing for joy." The question for us is what does that mean today? For me, that means I must remember the reason saints will sing for joy. Our salvation. There is joy in remembering our salvation. Even today as I am writing to you, the reminder of my salvation is such a comfort.

It gives me peace to remember, no matter what I am facing, my salvation is secure and in that truth there is joy. A deep and reassuring joy.

To remember my salvation reminds me of several things:

- My troubles are momentary compared to eternity.
- My wounds will be healed one day.
- I am forgiven.
- What seems urgent and stressful today is temporary.
- My Father in heaven loves me. He is here with me. He is my strength.

Take a few minutes to consider your own salvation and remember what gives you joy:

....

....

....

TUESDAY
IN LIGHT OF ETERNITY

Joy is promised to the followers of Christ. There is the joy of receiving the gift of salvation. We know that the Holy Spirit, living inside of us, produces the fruit of joy. There is also the joy of knowing we have a home in heaven and that we're on our way there.

Because of our salvation, we can keep eternity in view, sifting through the demands of today in light of where we are going. Would an eternal view help you to realign your perspective today? In light of eternity, what big things in your life would get new perspective? I'll start. . . .

In light of eternity, it doesn't really make sense to spend my money on a bigger house or a fancy shrub for our yard. When I remember eternity, I want to spend that money helping the children of God.

Now you go. . . . In light of eternity . . .

....

....

....

WEDNESDAY
CITIZENSHIP IN HEAVEN

Sometimes I will hear someone say, "I wish Jesus would come get us and take us all home." I understand why they say that. I have many days felt the same way, especially as a student before final exams! The heart wants to go where it was made to be. Heaven.

As Paul said in Philippians, *"our citizenship is in heaven"* (3:20). True, we are citizens of heaven, but until God calls us there, we are to live for His glory on this earth. And we are supposed to live in the promised joy given to Christ followers. Living that kind of life means that while we are on earth, we trust God for His promised joy. Looking for His joy. Celebrating His joy.

You are a citizen of heaven. Your salvation is secure. Now close your eyes and look for the joy of this moment. What do you see?

....

....

....

THURSDAY
SIMPLE JOY

My kids were on a mission trip to the mountains just last weekend. One of the aspects of the trip that impacted them most was the Christian folks' joy with their salvation, even though most of them live below the poverty level.

For the people in the mountains, their salvation brought all the joy they needed. They were living in God's promise of joy.

Are we sometimes too distracted by our things to remember the joy of salvation? To put our faith in God's promise? How does this verse speak to you today? *"Set your minds on things above, not on earthly things. . . . your life is now hidden with Christ in God"* (Colossians 3:2–3).

....

....

....

THE WEEKEND
SINGING FOR JOY

God promises that His followers will "ever sing for joy." I think that promise is supposed to shape almost everything we do while we're here.

Every day is obviously not filled with joyful circumstances or joyful relationships, and yet we can still have a deep, soul-joy. It's a promise.

How will that promise define your choices this weekend? Your time with your family? Your personal time? Shaping your heart? Since God has promised joy, where will you look for it, and how will you embrace it when you find it?

....

....

....

Joy is the flag you fly when the Prince of Peace is in residence within your heart.
—*Wilfred Peterson*

In the Presence of God

MONDAY
NOT SHAKEN

*Therefore my heart is glad and my tongue **rejoices**;*
my body also will rest secure,
because you will not abandon me to the grave,
nor will you let your holy One see decay.
You have made known to me the path of life;
*you will fill me with **joy** in your presence,*
with eternal pleasures at your right hand.
—Psalm 16:9–11

It's interesting that when King David wrote this psalm, he was in danger of death. But his words are not bitter, complaining, or gloomy. Instead, it seems like he has written from a deep place of calm and assurance. Being in the presence of God will do that.

The way David writes this psalm is the way I want to live my life. He was convinced of where his joy came from. He knew both desperately and confidently that no matter what he was facing, God was going to provide for his needs.

In the verse just before the scripture for today, we learn the reason for David's trust: *"I have set the LORD always before me. Because he is at my right hand, I will not be shaken"* (v. 8).

Don't you want to live like that? *"I will not be shaken."* Walking every day on this earth with so much trust that no circumstance, no bad news, and no brokenness can shake your confidence in God. That is exactly the kind of woman I long to be. That is the kind of faith I want to model for my children. That's what I want people to whisper behind my back, *"Nothing shakes her confidence in God."* See the progression of faith in verse 8 . . . because David always keeps the Lord before him, then he lives with a faith that cannot be shaken.

Now look at the fruit produced in the life of one who stays in the presence of God . . . *you will fill me with joy in your presence.*

Just like David, you and I will be filled with joy in the presence of God. It is both wisdom and delight for us to continually keep ourselves in His presence. To have the Lord always before us means that we keep our eyes on Him for every step. To count on Him to be as close as our right hand means we do nothing without His guidance.

To live in joy every day means to keep ourselves in the presence of God every day. Staying near to Him. In conversation with Him. Learning from Him. For the rest of this week, let's spend each day learning how to practice the presence of God. But first, would you pray with me? I'll get you started, then you finish:

Lord, teach me what it means to keep you always before me. Show me how to . . .

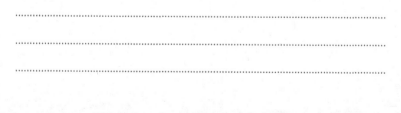

TUESDAY

MEDITATION

In the presence of God, we will be changed. The uncertain will be made sure. The empty will be filled. The immature will grow. In his book *Celebration of Discipline*, Richard Foster gives four inward practices that lead us toward the presence of God. Let's spend the rest of this week focusing on one practice each day. We'll begin with *meditation*.

To meditate is to give yourself the time and space to think. Not to ask. Not to tell. Just think. Ponder. Focus. Listen. God is continually speaking, and we want to hear Him.

Choose one of the following ways to practice meditation in the presence of God and then set aside a few moments today to begin.

- Meditate on Scripture. I love Foster's instruction "always remember that you enter the story [of the scripture passage] not as passive observers, but as active participants."[1] How about meditating on this passage for today: *"My peace I give to you"* (John 14:27).
- Meditate on creation.
- Meditate on the events of our culture.

What do you think Richard Foster meant when he said, "In meditation we are growing into what Thomas à Kempis calls 'a familiar friendship with Jesus' "?[2]

WEDNESDAY
PRAYER

Today we will seek the presence of God through *prayer*—the second practice Foster guides us toward. I love that becoming a person of prayer is a learned discipline. God meets you in prayer right where you are.

Many years ago, I wanted to teach several of my middle school girls about becoming more disciplined in prayer. We met together every week; and at the first meeting, I asked them to pray silently for five minutes. I even set a timer. About minute three, the wiggles began, but they made it. The next week I added five more minutes and so on. Eventually those girls were praying for an hour, finally realizing the beauty and ease of being in the presence of God.

Today, start where you are. Pray as simply as you need. Do not try to make your prayer life complicated. Just begin. Let God come to you. Linger if you can. We are in the presence of God when we pray.

Archbishop William Temple said, "The coincidences occur much more frequently when I pray." What "coincidences" have you experienced while in a season of prayer?

....

....

....

THURSDAY

STUDY

The third practice Richard Foster suggests that we integrate into our lives is *study*. In this book, we are spending an entire year studying little, tiny snippets of biblical joy. Every day you get another taste. Theologians might call what we're doing a "word study," which means taking one word and tracing it through every use and application in the Bible. I'm praying that this study about joy increases your appetite for studying the Bible. I pray that the interactions we have each day make you hungry for the word of God.

To study the Bible is to practice the presence of God. To study a book or verse of the Bible goes beyond meditation in that meditating is more devotional. Study is more analytical. When I am studying a passage of Scripture, I read how others have interpreted the verse. I pull out a map and look at the setting. I take notes and pray, asking God how to apply that truth to my life. Listen to what Foster has to say about study: "Study produces joy. Like any novice, we will find it hard work in the beginning. But the greater our proficiency, the greater our joy."[3]

In this book, we are studying joy together. Maybe today you can do your own extra study. Where in the Bible will you turn to add to your understanding of joy?

....

....

....

THE WEEKEND
FASTING

The fourth and final practice that Foster encourages us to observe is *fasting*. I had never in my life fasted until I was in seminary. And then once a year, our school required every student to participate in a mandatory fast. The entire student body fasted from lunch one day until lunch the next day. Twenty-four hours. That first year, I was scared to death. I had never really known anyone who fasted, and I was sure it would be the most torturous day ever.

Much to my surprise, several important things happened for me. First, abstaining from food for twenty-four hours really kept me focused on God. I had assigned a spiritual purpose to my fast and in those twenty-four hours I sought God more intently, even sensed His presence more acutely. Second, the physical aspect of omitting food for only one day wasn't really that hard. And third, I wasn't afraid of fasting anymore, especially when I realized the great benefit to my soul.

What if this weekend you fast just one meal? Please understand that there is no biblical law commanding regular fasting. But see what Jesus says in Matthew 6:16–18. Look up this passage and write down what you learn: "When you fast . . ."

....

....

....

Joy and laughter are the gifts of living in the presence of God and trusting that tomorrow is not worth worrying about.

—*Henri Nouwen,* Here and Now

WEEK 13

Is Not Found in Things

I denied myself nothing my eyes desired;
I refused my heart no pleasure.
My heart took delight in all my work,
and this was the reward for all my labor.
Yet when I surveyed all that my hands had done
and what I had toiled to achieve,
everything was meaningless, a chasing after the wind;
nothing was gained under the sun.
—Ecclesiastes 2:10–11

When I was in seminary, one of my Bible professors, Dr. John Martin, spent a couple of days teaching my class through the book of Ecclesiastes. By the time he was done, Ecclesiastes had become my favorite book in the Bible. I can still remember the deep, physical peace that God gave to me in that teaching. It was settled in my soul: what we do for God is all that matters on this earth. Period.

Several years later, I was meeting with some ladies and mentioned that Ecclesiastes was my favorite book. They were shocked. "But Ecclesiastes is so depressing," they told me. Obviously, they had not heard Dr. Martin's powerful teaching.

If there is one phrase commonly associated with Ecclesiastes, it's probably this one that's repeated through all twelve chapters: " *'Meaningless! Meaningless!' says the Teacher. 'Utterly meaningless! Everything is meaningless.'* " (Ecclesiastes 1:2).

I guess that could be a little depressing if you don't have the context. Wise King Solomon wrote over and over that everything under the sun is meaningless. Translation: there is nothing on this earth, absolutely nothing, that will give you the joy your soul longs for.

Some believe Solomon was a pessimist, but Solomon was not a pessimist or a cynic. He was a believer. The intent of Ecclesiastes is to shatter our confidence in all the things we do to find value. Solomon wants us to understand that faith in God is the only possible basis for meaning, value, and joy "under the sun."

No matter how many years you have lived, I bet you've already encountered that lesson many times. Accomplishments are great, but then what? A new house is wonderful, but what about something a little bigger? Last year's vacation was fun, but how will we top that this year? We can spend a lifetime running after the next little snippet of joy. Trying to manufacture enough of something to finally live in joy. Enough wisdom. Enough prestige. Enough pleasure. Enough wealth.

The book of Ecclesiastes offers us freedom! Freedom from trying to find "enough" so that we can live in joy. The answer we are looking for will never be found "under the sun." Solomon wants us to look "above the sun," where God is. He wants us to live our short years on earth putting our complete trust in God. Receiving and enjoying everything we have as a gift from the good hand of God. Living every single day in light of eternity, with our eyes fixed "above the sun."

It may seem like a big assignment, but I hope you can take the time this week to read through the 12 chapters of Ecclesiastes. As you come to your reading every day, do not allow yourself to read as a pessimist. Let these chapters set you free from useless striving. Keep your heart "above the sun" and let God speak to you about joy in this life.

Record here what stood out to you the most from chapter 1 of Ecclesiastes:

....

....

....

TUESDAY
ABOVE THE SUN

The older I get, the more I long for my life to have great purpose, and the more I realize that living my life for God's purpose is all that matters. Doing His will is where real joy comes from . . .

- loving my children for the glory of God, parenting them as He would have me parent
- building a marriage centered on our faith in God
- working with my hands and my mind on every assignment I am given in a way that makes God the centerpiece
- living each day with eternity in view

When we set our heart "above the sun," then we will find joy. With our heart set on God, then we are free to enjoy all that we have been given.

Today spend a few moments like this: Close your eyes and look at all you see in your life "under the sun." Now look up, "above the sun." Let God change your perspective. What do you see "above the sun"?

....

....

....

WEDNESDAY
MEANINGLESS EFFORTS

Solomon uses the book of Ecclesiastes to recount all the ways we try to find value and joy apart from God. When I read his words, I am reminded of all the time I have spent "trying" to make my own joy, and then I mutter his words to myself, "That was meaningless."

Look at the things Solomon calls vanity and see if you have spent some meaningless time too. The pursuit of toil, wisdom, righteousness, wealth, prestige, pleasure, youth, vigor, and even the future.

Take a minute right now to lay down all that is meaningless at the foot of the cross and leave it there, as you pray: *Lord, I don't want all that stuff. I want You. Your purpose. Your glory. Your joy. Amen.*

What meaningless efforts did you lay at His cross?

....

....

....

THURSDAY
FREEDOM FROM STRIVING

When I look around, I see a world that begs me to jump in and spend my energies trying to produce more things, earn more money, and accomplish greater feats. I have to confess that every once in a while, I have bought it. Go. Go. Do more. Run faster. Look to the left and the right. See where the competition is. Do it first. And do it better. All that is called striving, and I have felt it in my soul. I hate striving. It makes my stomach hurt.

Freedom comes to me when I turn to God and say, *I am Yours. I will work hard and study long, but only if it will bring You glory. God, what can I do that will bless You? Show Me Your purpose. I have already wasted so much. I only want Your plan for me. Use me for Your renown.*

Is there any striving in you? Solomon says it's like "chasing after the wind."

I pray we will both be free of the striving that steals our joy.

Write your own "prayer of freedom" here—a prayer that will slow your striving:

....

....

....

THE WEEKEND
FREEDOM TO ENJOY

In your Bible, read Ecclesiastes 3:1–14.

The ability to enjoy our lives is a gift from God. That joy will never come from things or endless pursuits. Only what God does will endure forever, and God wants us to understand these things so that we will revere Him.

May our joy over His gifts end all striving and bring Him the reverence He deserves.

What touched your heart or impressed your mind in the Ecclesiastes passage you read?

....

....

....

There is a joy which is not given to the ungodly, but to those who love Thee for Thine own sake, whose joy Thou Thyself art. And this is the happy life, to rejoice to Thee, of Thee, for Thee; this it is, and there is no other.

—*Augustine*, Works and Biography

For the Peacemakers

MONDAY

BECOMING A PEACE POSSESSOR

There is deceit in the hearts of those who plot evil,
*but **joy** for those who promote peace.*
—Proverbs 12:20

Blessed are the peacemakers,
for they will be called Sons of God.
—Matthew 5:9

I don't think I knew so much about peace before I had children. Moms make peace. It's one of our best things. I am such a peace-loving nut that I am always looking for ways to bring peace into our home. I light candles at dinner around the pizza box. I turn on music in the mornings so the kids can wake up calmly. I try my best to bend down and look into their eyes, especially when I'm redirecting an attitude. I get some quiet time with each child at night for a peaceful ending to the day. I want to make peace in our home, and I pray that God uses me to make peace in our hearts.

Do you realize that we are in a spiritual battle? Satan doesn't want our hearts to be at peace. He wants us to live underneath the weight of anxiousness, even making up things to worry about. He orchestrates sleepless nights and circumstances that feel like they might surely crush our peace. He wants us to operate in weakness so that our families bicker and argue, and marriages become mistrustful and full of suspicion. He wants to distract us from God; and if he can keep us fretful, without peace, he wins.

When Jesus said, "Blessed are the peacemakers," I'm absolutely sure that He knew we must have peace in our possession in order to give it away. We will not be able to make peace in our homes until we have become peace possessors. We have to own it. Live in it. Know what peace feels like. We must have the peace of God within us before we can promote the peace that gives joy.

Where are you in life right now? Feeling complete peace? On a path toward peace? Harboring a sense of foreboding and worry? Feeling anger rumble underneath the surface? Looking for peace in all the wrong places?

Let's take this week to seek the peace that leads to joy. First, consider this supreme road to peace: *"We have peace with God through our Lord Jesus Christ"* (Romans 5:1).

Peace was made when Jesus died on the cross. And peace becomes a part of our countenance through intimacy with Him. This week, let's intentionally pray about becoming peace possessors, so that we will have a peace inside of us to promote. Begin your prayer here. . . .

....

....

....

TUESDAY
THE PEACE OF GOD

We do not have to manufacture peace. I think I'd give up if I thought I had to dig down deep and find enough peace to sustain my life. I possess a degree of peace—but I'm always growing, always seeking deeper peace. I will possess peace because I have come to rest in my belief in God.

I trust that if I seek His will, God will not hide His direction from me. I believe in eternity and that gives me peace for these earthly days. I really believe that God works and reworks all things together for good. He restores what has been broken and heals what has been wounded. I don't possess peace just because I figured it all out. I possess peace only because I believe in Christ.

What is the source of your peace? Calm circumstances? A kind word? Money in the bank?

The Bible says that our peace comes from God and that when we promote His peace in our decisions and relationships, then we will have joy.

Take a few minutes to jot down some characteristics of the peace that comes from believing in Jesus:

....

....

....

WEDNESDAY
PEACE TRANSCENDS

Galatians 5 teaches that peace is one of the fruits of the Holy Spirit. Do you ever think about that? If peace is a fruit of the Spirit, then peace is the by-product of God being set free in our lives. The more room we have given Him to work in our souls, the more fruit we will bear in His name.

Peace is one of those amazing gifts that come from being in the presence of God. Look at what kind of peace Paul says we can have: *"And the peace of God, which transcends all understanding, will guard your hearts and your minds in Christ Jesus"* (Philippians 4:7).

A peace that transcends understanding is a soul-settling peace. A sleep-like-a-baby kind of peace. I believe when we possess the peace that transcends understanding, then we finally have something to give away. When we have a peace on the inside, then we will be able to make peace on the outside. Don't you want that kind of peace every day? I do.

Have you ever experienced peace that transcends understanding? When? What were the characteristics of that kind of peace for you?

....

....

....

THURSDAY
A PERSON OF PEACE

Look at a few of the phrases we might use to describe a person without peace:

Closes her eyes to injustice.

Keeps grudges.

Makes companions of those who lack integrity.

Runs from confrontation and resolution.

Looks for the negative in people and encounters.

Anxious and fearful. Expecting the worst.

Complaining. Whiney.

Prone to gossip and slanderous talk.

Self-centered and easily frustrated.

Now it's your turn. What words would you use to describe the person who lives in peace that transcends understanding?

....

....

....

THE WEEKEND
LIVING AS A PEACEMAKER

Questions for the weekend:

- Is there a difference between being a peacemaker and a peacekeeper? How would you define the difference?
- In Matthew 5, Jesus blessed the peacemakers. In the book of Proverbs, the peace promoters live in joy. What would make the difference in your life?
- Where do you need to become a peacemaker?

....

....

....

First, keep thyself in peace, and then shalt thou be able to be a peacemaker towards others. A peaceable man doth more good than a well-learned.

—Thomas à Kempis

In Between

MONDAY
THE DAY IN BETWEEN

*May the God of hope fill you with all joy and peace as you trust in him,
so that you may overflow with hope by the power of the Holy Spirit.*
—Romans 15:13

Today is the day in between.

The day in between death and life. The day of holy breath-holding. One more day of anticipation. Waiting. Praying. Hoping.

My whole family has taken a few days away at the beach this Easter. Yesterday was Good Friday, and appropriately the whole day was dark, cloudy, and cold. A deafening wind and rain began in the night. It was the kind of forceful rain that shook us out of bed and sent us around to check the latches and look in on all who were sleeping. There was a gate outside my window that kept pounding an eerie wail until we found a way to tighten it closed.

Good Friday night was just one of those nights when no

one slept well, and the dreary day that followed seemed a fitting reminder of the darkest day this world has known. Yesterday it felt like creation was remembering the darkness and
reminding us all to remember the day our Savior died to pay
for the punishment we deserved.

Today is the day in between. Tomorrow is Easter, but we
aren't there yet. Today we wait. All day I have thought about
the disciples who followed Jesus. On Good Friday, their
teacher died on a cross, he was placed in a tomb, and then a
rock was rolled across all the hope they had ever known. I can
only imagine the despair they must have felt.

Maybe that's what life feels like for you, too. Maybe you
are in between. Maybe a rock has been rolled across the place
that holds your hope and just maybe it feels like there is no
way your hope will ever be revived. When they buried your
hope, all your joy was taken with it.

If I could come and sit with you outside that rock, I would.
It's so hard to be in between. In between the death of a dream
and the rebirth of God's perfect plan. Waiting for what you
cannot believe God is big enough to do. Grieving. Mourning
what is lost. Weeping without hope.

Tomorrow morning, we're going to wake up early and
head down to the beach while it's still dark. The church up the
street is planning an Easter sunrise celebration and our family wants to be there. You see, the truth of Easter is the reason
you and I can wait in between. Jesus keeps His promises. He
said he would rise the third day, and He did. He promises to
give you a hope and a future, and He will.

This day, I pray that the God of hope, the God who rolled
away the stone, the God who was victorious over death, the
God who kept His promise—I pray that God will fill you with

a new hope as you remember His promise. And may the new hope of remembering restore your joy in this season of in between. May God whisper His truth into your soul . . . hope will rise!

Is there a tomb in your life where you have buried your hope and your joy? What have you buried there and how long have you been waiting?

....

....

....

⊙☞∽☜ ⊙ TUESDAY ⊙☞∽☜ ⊙
HOPE IN BETWEEN

Read Psalm 33:18–22. Do you know that the eyes of God are on those whose hope is in His unfailing love? Look at verse 19. Oh my goodness, God promises to keep us alive even during a famine! Are you living through a famine today?

Now take in verse 21. Why can you rejoice, even though life may feel like a famine?

....

....

....

WEDNESDAY
STRENGTH IN BETWEEN

"*Wait for the LORD; Be strong and let your heart take courage; Yes, wait for the LORD*" (Psalm 27:14, NASB). Today, what would it mean to be strong and let your heart take courage while you wait in between?

....

....

....

THURSDAY
WAITING IN BETWEEN

Read Mark 15:42–47. Maybe you feel something like Mary Magdalene and Mary the mother of Jesus. You have seen the tomb that holds your hope. Hope is gone. There is nothing alive. How do you imagine they felt on the day that Jesus, their hope, was buried in a tomb?

....

....

....

THE WEEKEND
HOPE WILL RISE

Read Matthew 28:1–10.
Oh hallelujah! Jesus is risen from the grave! He is alive! Our hope is not lost. Our joy can be restored.

How does the truth of Jesus' resurrection restore your joy today?

How about joy "in between"? Can you have a joy while you are waiting?

Where will your joy come from today?

....

....

....

Biblically, waiting is not just something we have to do until we get what we want. Waiting is part of the process of becoming what God wants us to be.

—*John Ortberg*

In Doing Right

MONDAY
CHOOSING WHAT'S RIGHT

When justice is done, it brings joy to the righteous
but terror to evildoers.
—Proverbs 21:15

He has showed you, O man, what is good.
And what does the LORD require of you?
To act justly and to love mercy
and to walk humbly with your God.
—Micah 6:8

Misery for me is knowing the right thing to do and then delaying. And then even worse, delaying so long I never do what I knew I was supposed to do. Oh, the torment I have brought to myself.

Do you know what I mean? The phone call you know you should make. The bill you keep meaning to pay. The dentist appointment you have put off. The relationship you need to mend. The project you began and then let drag out for months. Delay. Procrastination. Even downright disobedience. It's misery inducing. I have made myself miserable a hundred different ways, most of the time because I have known the right thing to do and instead of responding with quick obedience, I hemmed and hawed, thought it through, waited, and many times just froze. Solomon begins the book of Proverbs with a description of what the book contains, and in that short list is mention of "doing what is right": *"The proverbs of Solomon Son of David, king of Israel: . . . for acquiring a disciplined and prudent life, doing what is right and just and fair"* (Proverbs 1:1–3). Throughout the book of Proverbs, Solomon says there is joy in doing what is just and right. In my own life, I have proven that proverb over and over, so tell me why I would ever delay in doing right again. Sometimes it's fear. Sometimes insecurity. Sometimes it's busyness with less important things. And sometimes, it's probably laziness.

Justice or right-doing (righteousness) gives real pleasure. People who do what is right have a good and peaceful conscience. As far as they are able, they make God's will their will, and there is great comfort and stable joy in that kind of choosing.

If doing what is right gives us joy, then the obvious question becomes, why don't we choose the right thing as often as possible? Most of the time, I try to choose right. I bet you do, too. But other times I realize I have been afraid. Maybe doing the right thing would offend someone else, so I wavered. And then sometimes I have just been lazy. The right thing seemed like it might take too much of my time.

This week, choosing joy means that we examine the opportunities we have to do right. For today let's recommit our motives and actions. I'll begin by starting a prayer. You finish with your own words.

Father God, I do want to choose the right thing every single time I am able. With all my heart, I want my life to bring you glory. As I am learning to intentionally choose joy every day, doing the just and right thing is my heart's desire. Please forgive me when I have been hesitant or slow to obey. Please forgive . . .

....

....

....

TUESDAY
A WELCOME RECEPTION

As the prophet Isaiah says, God welcomes those who do right: *"You welcome those who find joy in doing what is right, those who remember how you want them to live"* (Isaiah 64:5, Good News). He is pleased when we find joy in doing what is right. When I consider my relationship with the Lord, I so desire that He would take pleasure in me. That my life would be welcomed by God. Do you see the picture of our welcoming God with His arms outstretched? Drawing you close? Smiling over you? Pointing you toward the very good thing He wants you to do?

You and I will choose joy when we do what is right. Let God show you what would please Him today. What good things is God leading you to today?

....

....

....

WEDNESDAY
TAKE IT TO THE HOOP

Many times my children will halfheartedly do the right thing. They will kind of get their dirty clothes to the laundry room, but not all of them. They will sort of help in the kitchen by taking their dish from the table, but not putting it in the dishwasher. For years I have said to them, "Take it to the hoop. Go all the way with the task you have been given."

When it comes to doing right, joy is the by-product of putting our whole heart into the work God has given. The apostle Paul put it this way: *"Whatever you do, work at it with all your heart, as working for the Lord, not for men"* (Colossians 3:23).

What will you take to the hoop today? Give your whole heart to, instead of only part? Do your work fully instead of halfheartedly?

....

....

....

THURSDAY
RESCUE FROM EVIL DISTRACTIONS

"*When I want to do good, evil is right there with me*" (Romans 7:21). Maybe you feel like the apostle Paul: you want to do good and live right but evil is right there with you. He goes on to say in verse 25 that Jesus can rescue us from the evil that keeps us from doing good.

Do you need a rescue today? Call on Jesus. Ask Him to remove any evil, any hindrance, any distraction that will keep you from the right living you long for. What distractions do you need rescuing from?

THE WEEKEND
FINISHING UP

Let's use this weekend to complete a few things. Many times, doing right means finishing some things we have left undone. Are there a couple of things you could finish in the next few days? Steps of obedience you might take toward choosing joy?

For myself, finishing means making a couple of relationship phone calls that have repeatedly fallen to the bottom of my list. It also means keeping a commitment I have made to one of my children.

Let me pray for us: *God, our intentions have been good, but many times our good intentions have been left undone. Lord, help us finish what you have called us to do so that we might choose the joy you give. Amen.*

Make a few notes here about what things you could finish this weekend.

....

....

....

Joy, not grit, is the hallmark of holy obedience.

—*Richard J. Foster*

WEEK 17

For the Rescued

I HATE THE DEVIL!

Joyfully giving thanks to the Father . . .
For he has rescued us from the dominion of darkness
and brought us into the kingdom of the Son he loves.
—Colossians 1:11,13

The seventy-two returned with joy and said,
"Lord, even the demons submit to us in your name."
—Luke 10:17

I hate the devil.

I hate him every day, but today my feelings are especially strong. Today my whole family has been keenly reminded that Satan is at work all around us. He is sneaky and yet blatant. Whispering and yet shouting. He doesn't give up or dial back or leave any of us alone.

The evil one has no new tricks, not one. And what amazes me is that the whole of mankind keeps falling for the same old things. We all do. I do. We let the devil walk into our homes even though he keeps wearing the same old disguises. He is like a cartoon character wearing glasses and a fake mustache, hoping no one notices he's in the room. I've had three wearying conversations in the past twenty-four hours. The kinds of things that would make any woman fall hard into despair. And I have to tell you, all last night while I slept, I could feel in my spirit the sickening approach of despair. Restlessness. Tears. Bad dreams.

It took me until this morning to recognize him. Gosh, why didn't I spot him sooner? It was this morning in my kitchen when I realized he'd snuck in, I spun around on my heels and declared, *It's you. You're so obvious now. How did I miss your shoddy disguise? Get out. O. U. T. Get out of here. You are messing with the wrong woman and the wrong family. Take all your slimy ways and all your evil talk and GET OUT OF MY HOUSE. I haaaattteeeee you.*

Next I made the rounds, walking into the bedrooms to pray for each one of my children. I stood at the front door and asked God to clean this place out. I can't stand the idea of knowing the devil has walked around in my house. *Oh Lord, we belong to you. Protect each one. Give us eyes to see evil and strength to avoid every ploy.*

I am not one of those people who is always looking for the devil. Maybe that's part of my problem. I forget about him. I forget that he's alive and well. At work in my world and in yours. Plotting. Deceiving. Tempting. He's just downright unrelenting and doesn't give up.

Maybe the devil has been walking around in your house too. Maybe he's been sneaky and crept in unseen. Here is the great news: Satan has been defeated because of Jesus Christ, and by His power you and I can stand against any of his evil schemes. But we will have to be aware and alert.

As we begin this week together, spend a few moments thinking about your family, your home, and your relationships. Has the devil been at work somewhere around you? If so, then spend some time in prayer, asking God to do what He has already promised to do . . . rescue you from the darkness!

....

....

....

TUESDAY
WE KNOW HIM BY HIS NAMES

Take a look at some of these names:

Accuser	Adversary	Deceiver
Enemy	Father of Lies	Lawless One
Liar	Power of Darkness	Tempter
Thief	Wicked One	Ruler of This World

We can know the work of Satan by his names. Is he at work around you?

Look at what the Bible instructs us to do: *In addition to all this, take up the shield of faith, with which you can extinguish all the flaming arrows of the evil one* (Ephesians 6:16). It's the *shield of faith* that protects us from the work of the evil one. In this passage, the apostle Paul tells us to "take up" the shield of faith.

An action is required. We have to consciously raise up our faith in the face of evil.

By prayer today, pick up the shield of your faith.

....

....

....

❧❧❧ **WEDNESDAY** ❧❧❧
THE SHIELD OF FAITH

Yesterday we read the Ephesians passage that instructs us to "take up the shield of faith." Here is the Bible's definition of faith: *Now faith is the substance of things hoped for, the evidence of things not seen* (Hebrews 11:1).

As you and I trust God to protect us from the snare of the evil one, we are placing our faith in the promises of God, many still unseen. I trust that God is big enough to rescue me and the ones I love from evil. I have faith that Jesus has already defeated Satan and that one day all evil will end.

What else does your faith tell you to trust about God?

....

....

....

THURSDAY
STAND STRONG

If that is the case, our God whom we serve is able to deliver us from the burning fiery furnace, and He will deliver us from your hand, O king. But if not, let it be known to you, O king, that we do not serve your gods, nor will we worship the gold image which you have set up (Daniel 3:17–18). When Satan (through the king) attacked the values and beliefs of Shadrach, Meshach, and Abednego, they were able to stand resolute and unwavering because of their faith.

Do you need to stand strong today? List the areas of your life where you need God's strength:

....

....

....

I'd love to pray for you. *Father God, we put our faith in you. And according to your promises, because of your Son, Jesus, we will stand strong today. In His powerful name, amen.*

THE WEEKEND
SHOULDER TO SHOULDER

In the days of the Roman army, the soldiers invented a very effective military tactic. When enemies began firing arrows, the Roman soldiers would stand shoulder to shoulder in the formation of a rectangle. Those on the outside would use their shields to create a wall. Then those in the middle would raise their shields over their heads to protect everyone from the fiery arrows. The result resembled an almost unstoppable human tank.

These are the days when we must stand shoulder to shoulder with the body of Christ. We are not alone and we do not have to stand against evil alone. What if we all raised our shields together! Jude exhorts us in verse 3: *to contend for the faith that was once for all entrusted to the saints.* We are powerful together.

This weekend I hope you can get some time with other believers who will stand with you against evil. You can raise your shields together! Use the lines below to write a prayer of faith and a prayer for the others who might stand with you.

....

....

....

I often laugh at Satan, and there is nothing that makes him so angry as when I attack him to his face, and tell him that through God I am more than a match for him.

—*Martin Luther*

In Spite of Evil

MONDAY
RESPONDING TO EVIL

*There is deceit in the hearts of those who plot evil,
but **joy** for those who promote peace.*
—Proverbs 12:20

About two weeks ago, I outlined several topic ideas and Bible passages I wanted to write about for this devotional. This morning I sat down to write and clicked my computer open to the topic I had previously assigned for today. When I reread the passage for this week, my jaw dropped open and my heart began to pound.

You see, last night my family stayed up until well past midnight to listen to the president of the United States. He reported to our country and to the world that terrorism mastermind Osama Bin Laden had been killed by military operatives in Pakistan. In my lifetime, Osama Bin Laden has represented the epitome of evil in this world. Now he is gone. Spontaneous celebrations of joy erupted all over the country. This morning the stories remembering his evil flood the news.

And at least for today, the hope for greater peace has given our entire country a new joy.

In my own life, I have had to make several decisions about the deceit and the evil I've run into. First, it is not my place to give consequences or to pay back evil. I have learned the hard way that the wiser judge is God. His consequences are enough. His vengeance is assured, and I do not have to concern myself with balancing the scales of justice.

Second, when I encounter evil, I have learned to get away as quickly as I can. When my spirit tells me that I am in the presence of evil, I leave. I have no desire to be where evil is or to allow its deceitfulness into my home. That means people, movies, video games, and any cloak that might try to hide the evil underneath. I don't want to go where evil is and I refuse to allow evil into my house. Our response to evil must be strong, adamant, and righteous. When you come up against the deceptive practices of evil, don't take a week to think about it. Take quick, effective action to separate yourself and your family from wickedness.

Third, my comfort and joy come from God. I am a follower of Jesus Christ; and as His follower, my aim is to live in peace as He lived. Even though I may suffer the wounds of evil, I can lay my head on my pillow every night knowing that my heart is fully devoted to God and His peace.

While we live on this earth, there will always be evil among us, but because of Jesus, evil cannot have us. We may be wounded. We may suffer the anxiety of too many encounters. But evil does not win. God does. Because we live inside the kingdom of God, forgiveness is possible. We who belong to the family of God live with the promise that evil has been defeated by Jesus' death on the cross. The victory over evil has been won and will be ours for all eternity.

Why don't we begin this week in prayer. I'll start and then you can continue with your own prayer:

Oh Lord, our God, I praise you for the hope and peace only You can give. Teach me to quickly recognize the deceit of evil and turn from it. Keep me safe in your righteousness. Let your Scriptures be my guide and my wisdom. Let me promote peace in my own heart . . .

....

....

....

TUESDAY
DO WHAT IS RIGHT

The book of Proverbs says that there is joy for those who promote peace. Today let's begin looking at Romans 12:17: *"Do not repay anyone evil for evil. Be careful to do what is right in the eyes of everybody."*

How will you actively choose not to repay the evil that your life has encountered? Why do you think it matters to do what is right in the eyes of everybody?

....

....

....

WEDNESDAY
PEACEFUL RELATIONSHIPS

Now for Romans 12:18: *"If it is possible, as far as it depends on you, live at peace with everyone."*

Living at peace requires a conscious decision. You decide to make choices that feed peace. What decision can you make for today's peace? If you tried to live a peace with everyone, how would that impact your everyday joy?

....

....

....

THURSDAY
LEAVE ROOM FOR GOD

Continuing in the passage in Romans, read 12:19: *"Do not take revenge, my friends, but leave room for God's wrath, for it is written: 'It is mine to avenge, I will repay.'"*

The huge burden of revenge has been lifted from your shoulders and transferred to God. Where in your life will you let God repay what has been done for evil? How will you intentionally choose to "leave room for God" and His wrath, instead of your own?

....

....

....

☙☙☙ THE WEEKEND ☙☙☙
OVERCOME EVIL WITH GOOD

The purpose of turning away from evil and leaving the consequences to God is to feed your own soul with Christlikeness. This weekend, how can you purposely practice this passage from Romans 12:20–21: *"If your enemy is hungry, feed him; if he is thirsty, give him something to drink. In doing this, you will heap burning coals on his head. Do not be overcome by evil, but overcome evil with good."*

There is great joy for the soul in choosing good. List three actionable ways you will choose to overcome evil with good:

....

....

....

❧ The Christian is cheerful, not because he is blind to injustice and suffering, but because he is convinced that these, in the light of the divine sovereignty, are never ultimate. ❧
                    —*Elton Trueblood,* Biography

WEEK 19

....

From Generation
to Generation

THE LEGACY OF A JOYFUL LIFE

One generation will commend your works to another;
they will tell of your mighty acts.
—Psalm 145:4

These commandments that I give you today are to be upon your hearts.
Impress them on your children. Talk about them when you sit at home
and when you walk along the road, when you lie down and when you get up.
Tie them as symbols on your hands and bind them on your foreheads.
Write them on the doorframes of your houses and on your gates.
—Deuteronomy 6:4–9

Last week, I went to my parents' house and loaded the back of my car with the dining room table and chairs that had belonged to my grandmother. There is still a sideboard and hutch to come, but we thought it was a miracle to get a full-size table and six chairs packed all around *me* for the five-hour drive home. An afternoon in the car, driving over the mountain with your grandmother's furniture creaking and shifting, gives a woman a little time to think about her heritage.

I asked for my grandmother's table because I vividly remember all the years of our family around it. The meals we ate and the games we played. The mess she always made in the kitchen. Her alto singing that plays in the background of every memory I have about her. But mostly, I remembered the great joy of being at my grandmother's house. While I was driving home, I decided that I wanted to pass the *joy* of being around her table to the next generations.

Maybe some would argue with this thought, but I believe the most powerful gift I can give to the next generation is a true and vibrant joy in the Lord. Joy. Even more than academics. Even more than experiences or inheritance. People who possess real and abiding joy will live powerfully and for the glory of God—no matter their purpose, calling, or path. From generation to generation, I long to leave the legacy of joy.

What if we allow ourselves to be transformed by the joy promised through the indwelling Holy Spirit? And then what if we intentionally teach our children, through spirit and deed, what it feels like to live a life full of joy? Could there be any greater gift to leave for the next generation? I think not.

We have lived in our house for three years and never once have we eaten a meal in the formal dining room. Not even a snack. Honestly, I don't think anyone has even had a conversation in that room, but things are about to change. I hauled a sixty-year-old table down the mountain so that every day we would remember. We're going to pull up our chairs, open the pizza box, and I'm going to tell my kids about their grandmother of great joy and the God that she loved.

Joy can become a legacy, but it begins today with you and me. We either choose to give the *things* we have been given or we choose to *live a life* that can be multiplied in others. Did someone leave you a legacy of joy? Who was it, and what do you know about joy because of them?

....

....

....

❧ TUESDAY ❧
SHAPING YOUR OWN LEGACY

Have you given any thought to what you'd like your legacy to be? What do you want people to say about you? How would you want them to imitate you?

....

....

....

❧ WEDNESDAY ❧
REJECTING JOY-LESS-NESS

Is there a cycle of "joy-less-ness" that needs to be broken in your life? We transfer to others what and who we are. Without an intentional choice to grow in joyfulness, a life without joy will be passed to the next generation.

What three things can you do to intentionally turn away from areas of joy-less-ness?

1. ....

2. ....

3. ....

THURSDAY
TRAINING IN JOY

Look at this Scripture and tell me what you think. *"Train a child in the way [joy] he should go, and when he is old he will not turn from it"* (Proverbs 22:6).

If the way you choose is the way of joy, does this ancient truth still hold?

....

....

....

THE WEEKEND
ENJOY THE JOURNEY

Leaving a legacy of joy for the next generation is about learning to enjoy every mile of this journey. Are you enjoying today? What about the miles you are currently walking?

In the next few days, spend some time thinking and praying about your legacy of joy and write here what God brings to your mind.

....

....

....

We were meant to give our lives away. Spend more time living your legacy instead of worrying about leaving it.
—Lee J. Colan

Instead of Despair

MONDAY

HOLY EXCHANGES

He has sent me . . . to bestow on them . . .
*a garment of **praise** instead of a spirit of despair.*
—Isaiah 61:1–3

The heart falls into despair when we forget. When we forget who we belong to and how very powerful God is. When the ways of evil seem to be winning and we forget that the victory has already been won by the Son of God, Jesus Christ.

In the book of Isaiah, the prophet says that God promises to make many holy exchanges for those who belong to Him. He takes mourning and gives comfort and gladness. He exchanges a crown of beauty for ashes. And for every one of us filled with a spirit of despair, God promises to exchange our despair for a *garment of praise*. A garment is a whole new outfit, not just a tiny handkerchief or a new tie. A garment is a complete covering. Only God could replace despair with a praise that becomes our joy.

This morning, I have asked the Lord, how do you do that? How can you physically, emotionally, and spiritually replace my spirit of despair with a garment of praise? Here is what I believe He has said to me:

1. Determine to take Me at My Word. Believe the truth you have been given.

2. Remember who I AM. What I have done. Who you belong to.

3. Look at your circumstances like I do. Recognize the deceiver. Do not allow yourself to fall into his snare.

4. In prayer, give Me your despair. You do not have to carry it anymore.

Not one thing has changed about the conversations I've had or the issues concerning my family. No one has called this morning to give me good news. But I can testify to you that my spirit of despair has been *exchanged*. I am praising God that discouragement does not have the final say and the tricks of the devil do not win. God is still able to do exceedingly, abundantly beyond all I can ask or imagine.

May this week be a week of holy exchange for us. I am praying that we will spend these next days trading every misery, anxiety, and disappointment for His life-giving praise and joy. If ever we needed to wear garments of praise and be filled with the fullness of joy, these would be the days.

Let's work our way through a short passage of Scripture this week and begin with this verse: *"If anyone acknowledges that Jesus is the Son of God, God lives in him and he in God"* (1 John 4:15).

Do you need to remember what it means to follow Jesus as

the Son of God? It means that God now lives in you and you in God. You belong to God.

No matter what fears or despair you face, you belong to God. Spend a few moments praying that truth back to God. Maybe you could begin something like this: *Lord, I belong to you . . .*

....

....

....

TUESDAY

RELYING ON THE GOD OF LOVE

The passage in John 4 continues. Here is our verse for today: *"And so we know and rely on the love God has for us"* (1 John 4:16).

I have fallen into despair when I have forgotten to rely on the love of God. Name three ways you can rely on the love of God today:

1. ....

2. ....

3. ....

WEDNESDAY
GOD'S PRECIOUS LOVE

The beautiful passage continues with these three precious words: *"God is love"* (1 John 4:16).

I have fallen into despair when I have forgotten that the very character of God is love. Concerning His character, God can never be other than He is. God can never act, react, give, or take in a way that is apart from His character of love. How has God been love to you?

....

....

....

THURSDAY
A LIFE WITHOUT FEAR

"There is no fear in love. But perfect love drives out fear" (1 John 4:18). God is perfect love and He is perfecting His love in us. As we grow in our understanding of who He is and the truth of His promises to us, His love for us drives away fear.

What fears or feelings of despair do you need the love of God to drive away?

....

....

....

THE WEEKEND
SURRENDER YOUR FEARS

"The one who fears is not made perfect in love" (1 John 4:18). It is common with God that to live in His power, a surrender is required. We turn to him and give Him our fears, our despair, and our aching hearts so that we might be perfected by love. So that a holy exchange can be made. So that we can wear the joy of the Lord like a garment of praise.

This weekend, what fears will you surrender to the God who wants to perfect you with His love?

....

....

....

I choose joy . . . I will invite my God to be the God of circumstance. I will refuse the temptation to be cynical . . . the tool of the lazy thinker. I will refuse to see people as anything less than human beings, created by God. I will refuse to see any problem as anything less than an opportunity to see God.

—*Max Lucado,* Upwords

In the Waiting Room

MONDAY
WAITING ON JOY

On my bed I remember you;
I think of you through the watches of the night.
Because you are my help,
I sing in the shadow of your wings.
My soul clings to you;
your right hand upholds me.
—Psalm 63:6–8

Yesterday, my daughter needed to see her ear specialist for an annual checkup. His office had relocated to a building attached to a hospital. On the way to his office, I guess we passed four or five different waiting rooms. Each one of those rooms was filled with patients and families, and with each one we passed, I remembered.

I remembered the surgeries our family has faced and the hour upon hour of waiting. I remembered the weeks of recovery, the visitors, the pain, and how it feels to wait for the unknown. Every single day, waiting rooms all over this world are full of people who have pressed Pause on their joy, collectively holding their breath while they wait. But you don't have to be in a hospital to be waiting. Even more of us wait in our daily lives, pacing on the inside, praying, hand-wringing, hoping. Delaying our joy until we have some answers.

But if our God has asked us to be joyful always, then where is our joy in the waiting room? Until the answers come? Before the promises are kept? While we wait for results and decisions and future plans? Where do we find our joy in the unknowns?

David wrote Psalm 63 from a desert in Judah while he was trusting God for an outcome he could not yet see. He called the desert "a dry and weary land where there is no water." Sounds like an Old Testament waiting room to me. Maybe you have known dry and weary seasons of life, where you, too, were waiting for answers, a road out of the desert, or a miracle that seemed slow in the coming.

Read Psalm 63 and then look at what causes David to sing:

First, he remembers that God is his help.

Second, he hides himself in the shadow of God's wing.

Third, David's soul clings to God.

Fourth, he trusts in the strength of God to hold him.

Are you in a waiting room today? Maybe you wait with your own questions or maybe you wait for someone you love. Maybe your waiting room feels like a dry and weary desert. For what does your soul wait?

....

....

....

◎◎◈◎◎ TUESDAY ◎◎◈◎◎
HELP COMES FROM THE LORD

When David began to sing in the desert, it was an out-pouring of joy. He sang because he thought about the Lord and remembered where his help comes from. *"My help comes from the LORD, the Maker of heaven and earth"* (Psalm 121:2).

Sometimes I have turned everywhere else before turning to the only true Help. Today write a prayer to the Lord, who is your help. Tell Him why you're waiting. Ask for His help in your wait.

....

....

....

◎◎◈◎◎ WEDNESDAY ◎◎◈◎◎
UNDERNEATH HIS WINGS

"Because you are my help, I sing in the shadow of your wings" (Psalm 63:7). When I close my eyes and envision myself in this passage, the picture is so very powerful. Me hiding beneath the wings of God. Safe. Protected. Loved. Do you need to re-member that you can hide beneath the wings of God today?

Hiding beneath the wings of God is a one-step journey. Here's how you do it . . . first, turn your mind, heart, and soul toward God . . . now *run to Him!*

Right there, beneath His wings, you can have joy in your waiting. Like David, you can sing.

Can you close your eyes and imagine yourself peeking out from beneath the wings of God? Keep that picture in your mind and then write down five words to describe how that feels:

....

....

....

∽∾∾∽ **THURSDAY** ∽∾∾∽
CLING TO YOUR GOD

David says his soul clings to God. *Cling* is such a powerful little word. It means:

- To hold on tightly.
- To adhere or stick firmly or closely to.
- To remain persistently or stubbornly faithful to something.

Use the above definitions of the word *cling* to write your own commitment to stay with God in your waiting:

....

....

....

THE WEEKEND

GOD IS BIG AND STRONG

In Psalm 63, David rejoices because he trusts that God is strong enough to hold him. Some days we need to be reminded of just how big and strong our God is. This weekend read Isaiah 40:21–31 and remind yourself about the strength of God.

No matter what you face . . . God is able to hold you with His strength.

No matter how long you have waited . . . He has not grown tired.

From the beautiful passage in Isaiah 40, what did you learn about God's strength?

....

....

....

Happiness depends on happenings;
joy depends on Christ.
—*Anonymous*

WEEK 22

In Surrender

MONDAY
PLASTIC PEARLS

Delight yourself in the LORD and he will give you the desires of your heart. Commit your way to the LORD; trust in him and he will do this.
—Psalm 37:4–5

My friend Marlene tells this story: There was a four-year-old girl who had been taken to the toy store by her mom. At the toy store, the little girl was completely enchanted by all the princess dress-up clothes and accessories. The little girl especially loved a necklace of plastic pearls, so her mother bought them for her.

The little girl insisted she always had to wear those pearls. She wore the pearls while she slept, in the sandbox, taking a bath. She never wanted to take them off. "I am a princess," she declared, "and a princess always wears her pearls." Months went by and over time those plastic pearls began to show their use. The string was dirty. The paint was chipping. The clasp had eventually been taped back together.

Every night before bedtime, this little girl crawled into her daddy's lap to snuggle and talk about the day. One night, her daddy asked, "Little princess, do you love me?"

"I love you, Daddy, I love you," the little girl joyfully replied.

"Will you give me your pearls?" her father asked.

"No, Daddy, they're mine. I'm a princess."

Her father kissed her on the forehead and the pajama-clad girl scooted off to bed.

The next night at snuggle time, her father asked the same question, "Do you love me?"

"Oh, Daddy, you know I do," the little girl responded.

"Will you give me your pearls?" he asked.

The little girl was adamant again, "Daddy, I am a princess," then quickly slid down and ran to her room.

The third night, the little girl, fearing the question that might come, was hesitant to snuggle with her dad. But love won out and the little girl rested her head on her dad's strong shoulder.

"Do you love me?" he asked.

Big crocodile tears fell from the little girl's eyes and, unable to speak through her tears, she nodded her head yes. The little girl loved her dad.

"Will you give me your necklace?" He calmly asked for the third night in a row.

That night the little girl ever so slowly unwound the tape that held her pearls together and obediently gave them to the father she loved. With one hand, her father took the strand of worn-out, plastic pearls and tossed them into the fire. With the other hand, he reached into his pocket and gave to his daughter a new strand of beautiful, real pearls. Exactly the kind that a princess should wear.

This week we'll talk about the plastic pearls in our lives.

Delighting in God, choosing joy, means learning to give everything to our Father, who can be trusted. Delighting means surrender. What stands in your way of *trusting* God with all you have and all you are?

....

....

....

⌘⌘⌘ **TUESDAY** ⌘⌘⌘
HOLD NOTHING BACK

The story about the little girl and her pearls has been rattling around in my head for several months now. As I remember its powerful illustration, the first question I ask myself is, *Am I wearing plastic pearls? Where in my life am I clinging to an imitation?*

How about you? Are you wearing any plastic pearls? Holding on so tightly that you may be missing God's better gift? Take a few minutes today to consider what it would mean to give all that is imitation to God. To keep nothing back. To open up and trust Him completely. He has great things in store for you: *"Open up before GOD, keep nothing back; he'll do whatever needs to be done"* (Psalm 37:5, The Message).

What would a string of plastic pearls represent in your life?

....

....

....

WEDNESDAY
TRUST BEYOND UNDERSTANDING

To delight in the Lord means to find our joy in Him. Don't you think the little girl delighted in the gift of her father? But before she could delight, he required her to give up her imitation pearls. In that surrender, she had to trust her father's good heart toward her. She had to believe, even when she could not understand, that his desire was for her best. She had to trust beyond her own understanding: *"Trust in the LORD with all your heart and lean not on your own understanding"* (Proverbs 3:5)

Where is God asking you to trust that His heart toward you is good?

What is God asking you to surrender?

Faith means trusting even when you do not have understanding. Is your faith being stretched today? You can pray and ask God to increase your faith so you can learn to trust Him more:

....

....

....

THURSDAY
GOD'S BETTER IS BETTER

I cannot count the times and ways in my life when I have held on to something I desperately wanted instead of quickly surrendering to receive God's better. The older I get, the more I want to quickly obey. I am learning that God's better is just that . . . better.

Jesus is talking about surrender when He says, *"For whoever wants to save his life will lose it, but whoever loses his life for me will find it"* (Matthew 16:25). He commands us to lose our lives so that we can live the new life He wants to give to us. For me, that means giving up anything that resembles my old imitation life and running after the new, real life I have been given in Him.

Sit for just a minute with your hands open, palms up, and let your heart pray a prayer of surrender to God. Tell Jesus that you are willing to lose your imitation life:

....

....

....

THE WEEKEND
THE JOY OF SURRENDER

Surrender is a big idea, but the picture of a little girl giving her dad a string of imitation pearls is such a beautiful picture of trust. I love that the little girl in the story wasn't quick to surrender her pearls. I have been slow, too. Because her daddy's gift was so lavish, I bet the little girl quickly gave the next time he asked.

The Lord has been lavish with us. Lavish forgiveness. Lavish love. Lavish grace. We have every reason to trust Him with what we deem valuable.

What if we learn to quickly obey? Quickly surrendering

anything He asks for and then trusting Him with what we cannot understand.

This weekend, spend some time in your Father's lap. A time of prayer. A walk in His creation. A longer time of study in His Word. Let Him tell you that He loves you, and then choose the joy of surrendering anything He lovingly asks you to entrust. What joys did you discover as you spent time in your Father's lap?

....

....

....

And so I urge you to enjoy this ministry of self-surrender. Don't push too hard. Hold this work lightly, joyfully. The saints throughout the ages have witnessed to this reality. . . . You know, of course, that they are not speaking of a silly, superficial, bubbly kind of joy like that flaunted in modern society. No, this is a deep, resonant joy that has been shaped and tempered by the fires of suffering and sorrow: joy through the cross, joy because of the cross.

—*Richard J. Foster,*
Brief Biography and List of Works

In Becoming Wise

MONDAY
CULTIVATING WISDOM

A man finds joy in giving an apt reply—
and how good is a timely word!
—Proverbs 15:23

According to this proverb, the joy that comes from wisdom has two parts: possessing wisdom to give, which is called an apt reply, then knowing when to give it, which is a timely word.

How many times have you known exactly the wisdom you should have given, three days too late. Or worse, maybe you blurted out bad advice when silence would have been more helpful. Knowing what to say and when to say it are the characteristics of very wise people. Knowledge is the accumulation of facts—and most of us spend years and money accumulating facts—but knowledge is worthless if it's incorrectly applied. The wise person finds joy in an apt and timely reply.

When I consider the people in my life who possess wisdom, each one of them shares many similar qualities:

gratitude	hopefulness	humility	dedication
integrity	concern	self-knowledge	openness
truthfulness	patience	curiosity	fairness
discernment	wonder	understanding	joy

We will become wise with the same measure that we cultivate the characteristics of wisdom in our own lives and hearts. Moreover, each proverb within the book of Proverbs is a statement of wisdom, and if we will choose to learn from those teachings, we will become wise.

Two Bible definitions will help us lay the groundwork for becoming wise. First, the definition of wisdom: *"The fear of the LORD is the beginning of wisdom, all who follow his precepts have good understanding"* (Psalm 111:10).

Next, the definition of "the fear of the Lord": *"To fear the LORD is to hate evil"* (Proverbs 8:13).

And so, for us to choose the joy of becoming wise, let us begin with an application of these definitions. To grow in wisdom requires that we examine our lives to make sure we have nothing to do with evil. To hate evil is more than merely disliking, it means to loathe, shrink back from, reject.

To grow in wisdom means that we take inventory of ourselves and then make intentional choices to turn away from anything that has even a hint of evil. Even as I am writing to you, I am praying, *Lord, show me if there is any evil in me. Any hint. Any mistake or laziness that has allowed a hidden evil. Please reveal to me everything that would keep wisdom away. And then give me the strength to obey quickly. Amen.*

If you have some extra time today, read Proverbs 8 with all its various descriptions of wisdom. Then spend some time examining your own heart. Is there any hint of evil that would keep you from becoming wise?

....

....

....

TUESDAY
ACCUMULATING WISDOM

Have you ever met a person who lacks academic degrees yet possesses the kind of wisdom most would gladly buy if they could? My grandfather, Cecil, was a man of great wisdom. Born in the Blue Ridge Mountains, he received very little formal education, but he built his life and his choices on the right ways of the Lord. All who knew him called him a great man of integrity. People came to talk with him when they had decisions to make. His commitment to the ways of God gave him a wisdom others longed to possess. The man Hosea describes in chapter 14 reminds me of my grandfather: *"Who is wise? He will realize these things. Who is discerning? He will understand them. The ways of the LORD are right; the righteous walk in them"* (Hosea 14:9).

Becoming wise means centering everything about our lives on the right ways of the Lord. And then staying there, year after year, accumulating the wisdom of a consistent walk with God.

Will you start or restart today with a centered, committed, unwavering pursuit of God's ways? What steps can you take to begin?

....

....

....

WEDNESDAY
PURSUING WISDOM

In Proverbs 2, we find out that becoming wise will require work. Solomon says this is how we are supposed to pursue wisdom: *"Look for it as for silver and search for it as for hidden treasure"* (Proverbs 2:4).

Choosing the joy of becoming wise requires intentional effort on our part. When I think about searching for hidden treasure, I imagine lots of research, maps, and study. Maybe finding the treasure requires years of hard work and digging, but when we desire such a valuable treasure, the work will be worth it.

How will you begin searching for this treasure called wisdom? I have a few thoughts to get you started:

- Spend intentional time with a person known for their wisdom.
- Track the word *wisdom* through all its mentions in the Bible.
- Join a Bible study or begin a study about wisdom.
- Read biographies of historically wise men and women.
- Commit to pray daily for God's wisdom in your own life.

Look at the list above and choose some ideas that will work in your life, or add some thoughts of your own:

....

....

....

THURSDAY
DESIRING WISDOM

"*Blessed is the man who finds wisdom, the man who gains understanding, for she is more profitable than silver and yields better returns than gold. She is more precious than rubies; nothing you desire can compare with her. Long life is in her right hand; in her left hand are riches and honor. Her ways are pleasant ways, and all her paths are peace. She is a tree of life to those who embrace her; those who lay hold of her will be blessed*" (Proverbs 3:13–18).

In the passage above, Solomon says that there is nothing you can desire that will compare to wisdom. Take a minute to circle the words in this passage that describe the person who becomes wise.

Now pray that God will make each one of those words true in your life, through wisdom:

....

....

....

THE WEEKEND
FOLLOWING A WISDOM MENTOR

I know a man who has a wide variety of life experiences and is full of the joy of the Lord. He was broke and in debt before writing best-selling books and then going on to lead several great companies toward their most successful years. One of his most beautiful traits throughout his seventy years has been that he has remained teachable in all that has come to him. He calls himself an early adapter, eager to be taught, thirsty to know more. Underneath all of his life experience, this man has kept himself faithfully committed to the teachings of Jesus Christ.

This man has accumulated much knowledge along the way, but because he passionately follows Jesus, his journey has made him wise. Many have recognized the value of his character and asked him to teach, so these days he spends most of his time mentoring, speaking, and writing. He is passing his notes back to help others learn to walk in wisdom.

Maybe you don't personally know a man or woman of great wisdom, but because of all the great technology, we can almost know them through blogs, podcasts, Twitter, and Facebook. I am currently downloading the sermons of Chuck Swindoll so that I can listen every time I am able. How will you pursue a wisdom mentor in your choosing joy?

....

....

....

Those who are wise will shine like the brightness of the heavens, and those who lead many to righteousness, like the stars forever and ever.

—*Daniel 12:3*

Through Forgiveness

MONDAY
REPENTANCE—THE PATHWAY TO JOY

*Restore to me the joy of your salvation
and grant me a willing spirit, to sustain me.*
—Psalm 51:12

Sin separates us from God. And when we have been separated from God, the very source of our joy has been cut off and removed. It is impossible to continue choosing sin and still live in the fullness of God's joy. Those two pursuits are mutually exclusive. Where you have one, you cannot have the other.

For the one who is choosing sin, there is no joy in the presence of God, only shame. Sin fills your spirit with darkness and shadows and there is an ever-present embarrassment and pain. The physical body trembles with anxiousness. The mind races, searching for ways to hide the obvious, hunting for a way out, an escape hatch, a jailbreak. Sin takes you prisoner, chained to the walls that separate you from joy.

King David committed adultery with Bathsheba and murdered her husband. His terrible and blatant sins separated him from God. Full of guilt and shame, David wrote Psalm 51 as his profound plea for forgiveness. This was his personal prayer of repentance, and it teaches us that repentance is the path from darkness back to joy. It's the road out of the pit.

The thing about sin is that no matter what variety or category or intensity, its presence in our lives will always separate us from joy. Choosing joy means that you and I must choose repentance from our sin as quickly and as often as it's required.

This week, let's focus on the repentance that restores God's joy in our lives. We'll use these next few days to walk through a little study of Psalm 51 so that its principles become familiar to us. I so desperately desire to live my years full of the joy of the Lord; and this passage is very clear: my repentance and God's gracious forgiveness will restore lost joy.

David begins his prayer with these words, "Have mercy on me, O God." Why don't we begin our week the same way. Let your heart remind you where you need God's mercy as you pray for God's mercy in your areas of need.

Have mercy on me, O God . . .

....

....

....

TUESDAY
NO SIN TOO GREAT . . .

In Psalm 51, David begins his turn toward repentance with a direct appeal based on the character of God: "*Have mercy on me, O God, according to your unfailing love, according to your great compassion blot out my transgressions. Wash away all my iniquity and cleanse me from my sin*" (Psalm 51:1–2). David appeals to God's *"unfailing love"* and *"great compassion."* Do you need to remember today that there is no sin too great to change God's unfailing love toward you? Don't miss this powerful truth. If an adulterer and murderer can call on the unfailing love of God, you and I, even from the depths of our sin, can turn toward Him.

Then David asked God, whose love never fails, to wash away all his sin. Repentance begins when we turn ourselves away from our sin and toward the Only One who can make us clean. What do you need to turn away from? Joyful restoration awaits you. . . .

....

....

....

WEDNESDAY
CONFESSION LEADS TO RESTORATION

After David turns toward God, he spends the next part of his prayer confessing his sin. He begins: *"For I know my transgressions, and my sin is always before me"* (Psalm 51:3).

I spend a lot of my spiritual energies trying not to sin. I don't want sin in my life. But sin is sneaky. It creeps in. And some days it's good for us to stop, search our hearts, and confess to the Lord both the sin we have chosen and the sin we have lazily allowed. Let's do that today. Just stop and bow your head. Let the Holy Spirit show you what to confess. Stay with this time of prayer as long as it takes.

....

....

....

THURSDAY

GOD CAN MAKE YOU *CLEAN*

When there is sin in us, we can do many things trying to make ourselves clean. Confess our sin to a friend. Seek professional counseling. Promise to do better next time. Perform acts of service to somehow pay for what we've done. All these things are good ideas, but none of them can make us clean.

We will be clean when we have been forgiven by God. David knew it was only the Lord who could make him whiter than snow: *"Cleanse me with hyssop, and I will be clean; wash me, and I will be whiter than snow"* (Psalm 51:7). All God requires is a remorseful heart. David understood this when he said, *"The sacrifices of God are a broken spirit; a broken and contrite heart, O God, you will not despise"* (Psalm 51:17). It's the same for you and me. Bring your regret to the Lord. It's only the Lord's forgiveness that can restore our joy.

Maybe you have been wandering around with your sin, looking for the right book or small group or seminar to set you free. My dear friend, just turn to God. He will wash you and make you clean. Right now, turn your heart and mind to Him, and write a letter to Him—a prayer—pouring out your heart like David did.

....

....

....

THE WEEKEND
TWO STEPS FURTHER

After David turns to God, confesses his sin, and receives God's forgiveness, he goes two steps further. David asks God to renew his heart and restore his joy: *"Create in me a pure heart, O God, and renew a steadfast spirit within me. . . . Restore to me the joy of your salvation and grant me a willing spirit to sustain me"* (Psalm 51:10,12).

Clean people make new commitments. David wanted to become steadfast in his spirit and to live in the joy of God's forgiveness.

As you choose the joy that comes from forgiveness, what new commitments do you want to make before the Lord? Take this weekend to decide; record some of your thoughts here.

....

....

....

Receive every day as a resurrection from death, as a new enjoyment of life.

—*William Law*

When Everything Is Gone

MONDAY
EVEN IF . . . WE WILL TRUST THE LORD

*Though the fig tree does not bud
and there are no grapes on the vines,
though the olive crop fails
and the fields produce no food,
though there are no sheep in the pen
and no cattle in the stalls,
yet I will rejoice in the LORD.
I will be **joyful** in God my Savior.*
—Habakkuk 3:17–18

Life has this way of bringing hardships we never expected. While I have been writing this book, tornadoes ripped across the United States. In a matter of minutes entire cities were devastated. Lives were lost. Everything was gone. A few weeks after the storm, I talked with an elderly lady at a conference where I was speaking. She told me that as the storm approached, her ordinarily unconcerned husband decided they should get in his truck and drive to the church to take shelter. When the storm had passed, they couldn't even get down the street to their house. When they were finally able to reach their house, everything was gone. Everything.

As she described the total destruction to me, I stood there in awe.

"Look at you," I said, "last week you lost all your worldly possessions, some of your neighbors lost their lives, and yet here you are today with this peaceful countenance, calmly telling me your story. I am amazed."

Then that tender old woman took me by the hand, leaned closer to me, and said this: "I have found out that when you lose everything, you still have the Lord."

The strength with which she said those words made me cry. She is right. Oh hallelujah, she is right.

I lived about seven years as a single mom, and during many of those first years it felt like the fig tree did not bud. There were no grapes on the vines. Life was overwhelming and everywhere I turned required more than I had. It was so very different from living through a tornado, but spiritually, emotionally, and mentally, it felt like everything was gone.

My dear friend lives several states away. Her family has not suffered the winds of a tornado, but the winds of a financial calamity have taken away everything she and her family owned. And the bills keep coming. And yet another child needs to see the doctor. And the life they were going to live is completely changed.

In his short little book, the prophet Habakkuk asks God two questions and receives his answers. Because of all he learns about the character of God, Habakkuk determines that even in the times of greatest fear, even if everything is gone, he will trust in the Lord and rejoice in Him. Habakkuk decided to choose joy.

This week, I pray that our circumstances will not define our choice. When everything is gone, the Lord remains. Like the prophet, may we choose joy. What circumstances threaten to steal your joy? What truths of God can help you restore that joy?

....

....

....

❦ TUESDAY ❦
OUR HOPE BELONGS TO THE LORD

Sometimes we misplace our hope. We can mistakenly put our hope in the wrong places. The wrong people. The wrong endeavors. When everything has gone wrong and when everything is lost, we will certainly lose our joy if we have placed our hope in those things. The writer of Psalm 42 understood this struggle: *"Why are you downcast, O my soul? Why so disturbed within me? Put your hope in God, for I will yet praise him, my Savior and my God"* (Psalm 42:11).

Our hope belongs to God. To choose joy when everything is gone requires us to give our hope back to God.

Today will you give God your hope? Fill in the blanks of this prayer:

Lord, instead of placing my hope in ....,

or ....

or ....,

I put my hope in you. I choose joy. Amen.

WEDNESDAY

THE LORD IS OUR STRENGTH

After the prophet Habakkuk chooses joy, he says this: *"The Sovereign LORD is my strength, he makes my feet like the feet of a deer, he enables me to go on the heights"* (Habakkuk 3:19).

Applying this passage to our daily lives might sound something like this:

When it feels like everything is gone, choose the joy of the Lord anyway. He will be your strength. He will give you the power to move joyfully through difficult circumstances. You will not live forever in the pit of low places. God will raise you up. Not only will God be your strength in the trials, He will take you up the mountain to victory and triumph.

My friend, who will give you the strength to choose joy? The Sovereign Lord is your strength. Finish this declaration of trust: *When it feels like everything is gone, I choose the joy of the Lord anyway, because . . .*

....

....

....

THURSDAY

WHEN LIFE SHAKES OUR STRENGTH

In Psalm 9:13–14, David said, *"O LORD, see how my enemies persecute me! Have mercy and lift me up from the gates of death, that I may declare your praises . . . and . . . rejoice in your salvation."*

A modern-day translation of this passage might sound something like this:

> O Lord, see how my children ignore me.
> See how my husband mistreats me.
> See how my finances devastate me.
> See how my body betrays me.

Do you have a modern-day translation of this passage that would apply to your own life? Write your interpretation below:

....

....

....

THE WEEKEND
JOY RESTORED

Notice the pattern in the passages we've studied this week:

Overwhelming circumstances.

Hope is lost.

Choosing God despite troubles.

Joy restored.

This weekend I want you to look for an opportunity to apply this pattern to your everyday life and any trouble you might face. We can choose joy when it seems like everything else is gone. What application of this pattern do you see in your life?

....

....

....

....

❦ I don't think of all the misery but of the beauty that still remains. ❧

—*Anne Frank*

JOY

In Worship

WHAT IF YOU COULD SEE?

Worship the LORD with gladness;
*come before him with **joyful** Songs.*
—Psalm 100:2

Praise the LORD. Sing to the LORD a new Song, . . .
*Let Israel **rejoice** in their Maker; . . .*
Let them praise his name with dancing
and make music to him with tambourine and harp.
For the LORD takes delight in his people;
he crowns the humble with salvation.
Let the saints rejoice in this honor
*and sing for **joy** on their beds.*
—Psalm 149:1–5

Imagine this. What if God pulled back the veil for just a peek?
What if He decided to stretch His mighty hand over to pull
back the veil that hangs between us and the realm of the unseen? What if we could see with spiritual eyes for just a minute?

What if we could glimpse God seated on the throne of all creation? We'd see His Sovereignty. That nothing on this earth is unseen by Him. That He is powerful and glorious. That all the created bow to Him.

What if we saw the Father's love in His eyes? Our names written on His palm. Jesus, our Savior, at His right hand. The Holy Spirit interceding, day and night, praying for us by name, never ceasing.

What if you could see the angels sent to camp all around you, ministering to you and protecting you? What if you could look over and see your clean slate of forgiveness? The grace that runs downhill to cover you? The miracles performed on your behalf?

What if just for a moment you could see? What would you do? How would that change things for you? Would you obey a little faster? Serve with greater passion? Love with all your being? Would you choose the joy of spending your life worshiping the Only One who is worthy?

I think that if we could see, we'd fall to our knees in worship. With only a glimpse, we'd be changed. Worship would become our purpose, our joy, our ministry, and our service. We'd worship God with a fierce love for all people. A passion for the work He has given to us. We'd keep ourselves in His presence. Going as He says go. Waiting when He says wait. Keeping ourselves filled with the powerful presence of His Spirit.

This week, let's ask God for spiritual eyes to see. If only a peek, we want to see His glory. And let's choose the joy of worshiping our everlasting God.

Today, let's begin with a purposeful quiet. Wherever you are, find some way or some place you can be still. Then I want you to be still long enough to know God is with you. He is present. He is with you.

Read the following verse: *"Be still, and know that I am God;
I will be exalted among the nations, I will be exalted in the earth.
The LORD Almighty is with us"* (Psalm 46:10–11). Now think
about a place and a time of day when you can be still before
God—write it down.

....

....

....

TUESDAY

WORSHIP IN TRUTH

"*Yet a time is coming and has now come when the true worshipers will worship the Father in spirit and truth, for they are the
kind of worshipers the Father seeks. God is spirit, and his worshipers
must worship in spirit and in truth*" (John 4:23–24). In the pre-
ceding verse, Jesus is calling us to two things: worship that is
sincere and worship centered on His truth to us in His Word.

In this world of distractions and busyness, how will we become sincere worshipers? We will ask the Lord to make us
sincere. Reverent. Committed. Passionate. When I remember
who God is instead of focusing on myself, perspective quickly
returns about who I am called to worship.

Worshiping God in truth means centering my life and my
practices on the solid teaching of the Bible. When we devote
ourselves to the study of God's Word, we will stay centered.
Our minds will build a biblical grid through which to fil-
ter any teaching or forms of worship. Knowing the Bible will
cause us to worship in truth.

What biblical truths do you know that guide you in how to worship?

....

....

....

WEDNESDAY

WORSHIP—BOTH PRIVATE AND CORPORATE

The joy of *private* worship can be ours: *"On my bed I remember you; I think of you through the watches of the night. Because you are my help, I sing in the shadow of your wings"* (Psalm 63:6–7).

And the joy of *corporate* worship can be ours: *"I will extol the LORD with all my heart in the council of the upright and in the assembly"* (Psalm 111:1).

Choosing joy means that we worship God both privately and with others. I love the Lord with all my heart. I am a student of His word. I spend time with Him in prayer daily. I attend worship services with my church and others. But only recently have I been learning about an intentional time of private worship every day. For me that has meant spending part of my prayer time in worship. Or taking a walk and quietly speaking my worship to God. Sometimes I sit quietly and worship through music.

How will you privately worship the Lord today?

....

....

....

THURSDAY
WORSHIPING IN REVERENCE AND AWE

Thankfulness leads us to worship the Lord with reverence and awe, as we see in this passage from Hebrews: *"Therefore, since we are receiving a kingdom that cannot be shaken, let us be thankful, and so worship God acceptably with reverence and awe for our 'God is a consuming fire' "* (Hebrews 12:28–29). Reverence means sincerity. To worship with awe means struck with wonder, filled with joy!

Spend some time writing your thankfulness below. Then allow your grateful heart to show you how to worship God this day with reverence and awe!

....

....

....

THE WEEKEND
FAITHFULLY AND IN TRUTH

"Come, let us bow down in worship, let us kneel before the LORD our Maker; for he is our God and we are the people of his pasture, the flock under his care" (Psalm 95:6–7). There are many, many ways to choose the joy of worship. Praying God's Word. Singing God's Word. Observing the Holy Sacraments of God's Word. I think the overarching intent of Scripture is that we faithfully worship the Lord with sincerity based on His truth.

This weekend, to choose joy, can you do these two things: Intentionally worship the Lord privately. Intentionally worship the Lord with others. Record some thoughts from your worship here:

....

....

....

The most valuable thing the Psalms do for me is to express the same delight in God which made David dance.

—C. S. Lewis

WEEK 27

In Affliction

EVEN IN OUR AFFLICTION

*Be **joyful** in hope, patient in affliction, faithful in prayer.*
—Romans 12:12

*Be alert servants of the Master, **cheerfully** expectant.*
Don't quit in hard times; pray all the harder.
—Romans 12:12 The Message

Several years ago I attended church with a woman who has reshaped my spiritual walk forever. About thirty years my senior, this dear woman of God was diagnosed with breast cancer, a very serious and progressive cancer that the doctors wanted to attack with rigorous and difficult treatment. Surgeries, daily chemotherapy, and radiation ensued.

This precious woman decided to choose joy in her affliction. Every visit to the doctors and nurses became an opportunity for her to minister to them. When her hair began to fall out, she took all of her grandchildren to the hair salon and threw a party for the salon upon the occasion of her new wig selections. Cake, balloons, and streamers were included. My sweet friend could not tolerate the antinausea medication, so the chemo kept her excruciatingly sick. There were many midnight runs to the emergency room. Nausea on the side of the road and almost intolerable fatigue. But every single day of her journey, this woman chose lavish and heartfelt joy.

After several years of treatment, my friend has beaten her cancer. And everyone who knows her, including me, has learned a lesson that changed us. As I watched the months go by and heard the testimony of her spirit, I began to pray, *Oh Lord, no matter what comes to me, make me like her. Let me be a living witness to your powerful Holy Spirit.*

Theologians tell us that affliction is the occasion for calling forth our Christian virtues. In our affliction, we are supposed to reflect the character of Christ in us. To be joyful in hope, patient in affliction, and faithful in prayer is the way a follower of Christ chooses joy even in the most devastating circumstances.

In my old nature, there is no way I could have chosen joy like my friend with breast cancer. But God is changing me. His Spirit is working inside of me. I yearn to be a woman of joy, even when there is affliction.

Let's begin with our nature. God promises that the old will be made new: *God, take my old nature and replace it with a spirit of joy. For your glory, I long to change. Amen.*

What in your nature do you long for God to replace with joy?

....

....

....

⊙~⊸⊶⊸ **TUESDAY** ⊙~⊸⊶⊸
VIGILANT IN HOPE

"*We have peace with God through our Lord Jesus Christ, through whom we have gained access by faith into this grace in which we now stand. And we rejoice in the hope of the glory of God*" (Romans 5:1–2).

Even in our affliction, Jesus promises we have the hope of God. Hope is ours because we belong to Him!

"*Praise be to the God and Father of our Lord Jesus Christ! In his great mercy he has given us new birth into a living hope through the resurrection of Jesus from the dead*" (1 Peter 1:3).

To be joyful in hope is to keep hope in mind. To let hope be the banner hanging across your life. We must be vigilant in keeping hope in sight because this world will try to distract us.

Take the Bible passages from today and pray them back to God as your personal prayer of thanksgiving. You have hope.

....

....

....

⊙~⊸⊶⊸ **WEDNESDAY** ⊙~⊸⊶⊸
HOPE DOES NOT DISAPPOINT

"*We rejoice in the hope of the glory of God. Not only so, but we also rejoice in our sufferings, because we know that suffering produces perseverance; perseverance, character; and character, hope. And hope does not disappoint us, because God has poured out*

his love into our hearts by the Holy Spirit, whom he has given us"
(Romans 5:2–5).

We can have joy because hope does not disappoint us in
our afflictions. As a matter of fact, hope keeps rising within us
as we persevere in spite of our afflictions. That no matter what
has come to us, we keep going deeper with God. We keep
choosing joy. We keep rejoicing.

What disappointments have come into your life that
wilted your joy? Perhaps you are experiencing a disappointment now. Ask God to revive your joy as you rely on His
promises:

....

....

....

THURSDAY
HOLD ON TO HOPE

*"But Christ is faithful as a Son over God's house. And we are his
house, if we hold on to our courage and the hope of which we
boast"* (Hebrews 3:6).

Choosing joy in our affliction means holding on to our
courage because we belong to the house of Christ. There is
nothing more powerful than watching a fearful person be
transformed because she remembers to whom she belongs. We
are not commanded to be brave all by ourselves. We are made
courageous because of Christ in us. We trust His character.
We believe His promises. We turn to Him for our hope.

Maybe you haven't ever been very courageous. Do you

know that even in your affliction, the spirit of Jesus Christ can make you brave?

How do you need to be brave today? Ask God. He gives strength to the weak.

....

....

....

THE WEEKEND

ALL THINGS WORK TOGETHER FOR GOOD!

"*And we know that in all things God works for the good of those who love Him*" (Romans 8:28).

My friend with cancer never waivered on this truth. She believed that in her sickness, God was working all things for good. Through her appointments and endless testing, God was still working for good. In the years of pain and fatigue, God was working.

My sister persevered in hope and that hope produced great and abundant joy. Not only for her, but for everyone who had the privilege to be in the same room with her.

What are the afflictions that concern you? List as many as you can below:

....

....

....

Above, where you have written your afflictions, now boldly write these words: *I choose joy because I have hope that God is working in all these things for good.*

There are souls in this world which have the gift of finding joy everywhere and of leaving it behind them when they go.
                            —*Frederick William Faber*

In the Holy Spirit

For the kingdom of God is not a matter of eating and drinking,
but of righteousness, peace and joy in the Holy Spirit.
—Romans 14:17

Jesus, full of joy through the Holy Spirit.
—Luke 10:21

There is a difference in the person who is saved and getting by as best she can and the person who is saved, living every day of her life filled with the power of the Holy Spirit. The first person is living a carnal life. The second one is spiritual. Each of us receives the Holy Spirit when we believe that Jesus is our Savior and choose to follow Him with our life. It is the Holy Spirit who makes us spiritual.

The first person has asked Christ to be her Savior but continues to walk according to old desires. The second person is being led by the Spirit of God. There is only one degree of choosing that separates the two. But as it turns out, one degree makes all the difference.

At the beginning of our new lives with Jesus, we are spiritual babies, but as followers of Christ, we are called to grow up in our faith, to become spiritually mature. Becoming spiritually mature requires that one degree of choosing. The one who is becoming spiritual is being filled and refilled by the powerful presence of the Holy Spirit. The abundant, full life that Christ promises comes to us from the full indwelling of the Holy Spirit in us: *"I have come that they may have life, and have it to the full"* (John 10:10).

Spiritual maturity is the process by which Christ in us begins to subdue our old sin nature, and we become more in tune with the Holy Spirit. As we grow spiritually, the fruit of the Holy Spirit becomes more evident in our lives. Old sins lose their hold. We grow in our faith and live more fully devoted lives.

There is a difference between the presence of the Holy Spirit and the fullness of the Holy Spirit, where spiritual maturity happens. When we live in such a way as not to quench the work of the Holy Spirit, spiritual maturity happens in us. There is great, great joy in allowing the Holy Spirit to grow us into mature followers of Christ.

Let's spend this week looking at the Scripture's teaching about the Holy Spirit. First: *"Peter replied, 'Repent and be baptized, every one of you, in the name of Jesus Christ for the forgiveness of your sins. And you will receive the gift of the Holy Spirit. The promise is for you and your children and for all who are far off—for all whom the Lord our God will call' "* (Acts 2:38–39).

When you turn from your sin to follow Jesus, two things happen: Jesus forgives you of your sin, and the Holy Spirit comes to live inside of you. That promise is for all who turn to God.

Let me begin a prayer for us today:

God, thank you that the Holy Spirit lives inside of me. I want that one degree of difference. I want to live my life listening to His leading. Obeying the Spirit's guidance. Living in the fullness of your promise to me. I choose the joy of the Holy Spirit. Amen.

Now, you continue on—sharing your desire to follow and obey the Spirit:

....

....

....

TUESDAY
THE PROMISE IS FOR YOU

Do you remember the disciples and the three years they spent with Jesus on this earth? They did not yet have the Holy Spirit, and what we most remember about them in those years is their weakness, their lack of confidence and their struggles with pride. They gave up on the Savior, denied Him, fell asleep on Him, and fought over who would be the greatest.

The night he was betrayed, Jesus promised the disciples (and us) the Holy Spirit: *"I will ask the Father, and he will give you another Counselor to be with you forever—the Spirit of truth. The world cannot accept him, because it neither sees him nor knows him. But you know him, for he lives with you and will be in you"* (John 14:16–17).

In our weakness and pride and lack, Jesus has sent the Holy Spirit for us too. He lives inside of you now—guiding you, never leaving you. What weaknesses and lack will you surrender to Him as He helps you grow in joy?

....

....

....

WEDNESDAY
CHANGED BY THE SPIRIT

On the Day of Pentecost, the promised Helper called the Holy Spirit came to live inside of the disciples. *"All of them were filled with the Holy Spirit"* (Acts 2:4).

After the Spirit of God came to fill the disciples, the rest of the book of Acts testifies to the radical difference this new power made in their lives. Darkness was removed. They were made holy. The timid and fearful disciples became humble, bold servants of Christ. The bickering ended, and they became unified in spirit and purpose.

Too many times I have been a fearful, whimpering disciple, but the power of the Holy Spirit can change me. There will be joy in our lives as we are being changed, becoming spiritually mature, full of the Spirit of God. What changes have you already seen in your life as a result of the Spirit's presence?

....

....

....

THURSDAY
JESUS—THE CENTER OF OUR LIVES

The one degree between carnal and spiritual is a choice. When we choose to keep Jesus at the center of our lives, the Holy Spirit is set free to work and fill our lives with spiritual things.

When we keep Jesus on a shelf or off to the side of our lives, the Holy Spirit will be quenched—present, but not working. We will become stale, without power, operating in our weakness, not in the fullness of God.

Oh God, let all of my life, my thoughts, my actions, my heart, be centered on your Son, Jesus Christ.

Ask God to set the Holy Spirit free in your life to shape you, guide you, make you more like Christ:

....

....

....

THE WEEKEND
THE BLESSING OF BEING REFILLED

I am always asking the Lord to reveal any part of me that might hinder or quench the presence of the Holy Spirit inside of me. I Thessalonians 5:19 says, *"Do not put out the Spirit's fire."*

Thankfully, over and over, you and I can be made clean. Forgiven. We can choose to obey God and be refilled.

Charles Ryrie said:

The most distinguishing feature of filling [by the Holy Spirit] *is that it is a repeated experience. . . . That it can be repeated is a blessing, for if it were not so, no believer would remain filled for long, since sin breaks the control of the Spirit.*

This weekend, choose the joy of the Holy Spirit. Choose one degree of difference. Realign every area of your life so that your focus is entirely Jesus. Spend a moment listing the areas of your life that you will ask God to realign; then ask Him.

....

....

....

◖ *Spirit-filled souls are ablaze for God. They love with a love that glows. They serve with a faith that kindles. They serve with a devotion that consumes. They hate sin with a fierceness that burns. They rejoice with a joy that radiates. Love is perfected in the fire of God.* ◗
—*Samuel Chadwick,* Biography

Because of Heaven

MONDAY
REJOICE IN THE PROMISE

However, do not rejoice that the spirits submit to you,
*but **rejoice** that your names are written in heaven.*
—Luke 10:20

***Rejoice** and be glad, because great is your reward in heaven.*
—Matthew 5:12

Sometimes I'll hear someone say, "I wish Jesus would just come back and get us all. I'm ready to get out of here." I understand why they say that. We'll be home when we get to heaven. Finally healed—body, soul, and mind. The striving will cease. There will be no more bills to pay. Tests to take. Disappointments to weather. Evil and all its torment will be thrown into a lake of fire. We will have an eternity of fellowship, worship, service, and joy. Heaven sounds really good to me today.

But we live this day in the now and not yet. Heaven is our promise. Earth is our assignment. According to Jesus, we can choose the joy of heaven today. We can live with heaven in view, so that the joy of heaven fills our souls and gives strength to our hearts.

Remembering that my name is written in heaven gives an immediate peace to my countenance. This morning I made a list of all that needs to be accomplished before noon, but as I read that beautiful truth, that *my name is written in heaven*, the Lord calmed my heart and reminded me that one day there will be no more overwhelming lists. Because of heaven, I can choose joy in all that is assigned to me today. It will not have me forever; I'm going home.

This week, let's turn our hearts toward heaven and choose to live every day rejoicing in the promise of our eternal home. I imagine that you are a lot like me and you can feel your heart longing for eternity and your home in heaven. Spend some time today journaling your heart. What do you most long for about heaven?

....

....

....

TUESDAY
HEAVEN IN VIEW

When I keep heaven in view, then I have so much more perspective about my struggles on this earth. The joy of heaven gives me strength to endure. Even this physical body that is beginning to show its wear will one day be made new. Paul said, *"But our citizenship is in heaven. And we eagerly await a Savior from there, the Lord Jesus Christ, who, by the power that enables him to bring everything under his control, will transform our lowly bodies so that they will be like his glorious body"* (Philippians 3:20–22).

Whatever ailments or struggles you face in your own body, would you let the truth of heaven refresh your spirit? Our lowly will be made glorious. Our weakness will be gone. Fatigue will be banished. Today I am going to choose the joy of heaven. It will be amazing to trade this aching, earth suit for glory! Keeping heaven in your mind, what new perspective do you have about your struggles here on earth?

....

....

....

WEDNESDAY
THE OLD ORDER WILL PASS AWAY

"*And I heard a loud voice from the throne saying, 'Now the dwelling of God is with men, and he will live with them. They will be his people, and God himself will be with them and be their God. He will wipe every tear from their eyes. There will be no more death or mourning or crying or pain, for the old order of things has passed away'* " (Revelation 21:3–4).

Read the description of heaven above. Use the space below to rewrite each promise God makes to you in the passage. I'll get you started:

The dwelling of God will be with me.
He will live with me.

....

....

....

THURSDAY
THE URGENCY OF SHARING JESUS

In his book *The Noon Day Devil*, C. S. Lewis writes about three devils arguing heatedly about how best to win souls for Beelzebub. One devil says, "Tell them there is no God." The next devil says, "Tell them there is no Heaven." But the third devil, who is older and wiser, says, "Better yet, tell them there is no hurry. There'll be plenty of time later to do the work of the Lord."

Choosing joy because of heaven is such a powerful reminder about our urgency here on earth. Sooner than we realize, our joy will be complete in heaven. But while we are still here, so many need to know about Jesus.

Let the joy of heaven spill, my friend. Don't delay in telling those you meet about our Savior and our promised home. Who in your life do you need to share Jesus with? How and when will you do it?

....

....

....

THE WEEKEND
UNTIL HEAVEN

"*Then the angel showed me the river of the water of life, as clear as crystal, flowing from the throne of God and of the Lamb down the middle of the great street of the city. On each side of the river stood the tree of life, bearing twelve crops of fruit, yielding its fruit every month. And the leaves of the tree are for the healing of the nations. No longer will there be any curse. The throne of God and of the Lamb will be in the city, and his servants will serve him. They will see his face, and his name will be on their foreheads. There will be no more night. They will not need the light of a lamp or the light of the sun, for the Lord God will give them light. And they will reign forever and ever. The angel said to me, 'These words are trustworthy and true' "*(Revelation 22:1–6).

I cannot wait to get there! But until we get to heaven, let's lay hold of everything God has for us on this earth. Let the joy of heaven renew your compassion. Deepen your love for others. Remind yourself what matters forever and what doesn't matter at all. Open your heart to new ideas, new people, and new adventures. And may the hope of heaven settle a peace deep within us so that we live here on earth in peace.

Reread the scripture we opened with today. What grabs at your heart and makes you say *YES!* Journal your thoughts here:

....

....

....

A short stay here on earth will make heaven all the more heavenly.
—Charles Haddon Spurgeon

When You Are Waiting

MONDAY
THE COURAGE TO WAIT

"Jehoshaphat appointed men to sing to the LORD and to praise him for the splendor of his holiness as they went out at the head of the army, saying: 'Give thanks to the LORD, for his love endures forever.' . . . Then, led by Jehoshaphat, all the men of Judah and Jerusalem returned joyfully to Jerusalem, for the LORD had given them cause to rejoice."
—2 Chronicles 20:21,27

The story of Jehoshaphat is one of my favorite Old Testament stories. Jehoshaphat was a man of God. He sought the Lord for direction. He led as God instructed. But after all those things, Jehoshaphat and his people found themselves under attack from a vast army. The Bible says that when they saw the army coming, and with no power to protect themselves, Jehoshaphat cried out to the Lord, *"We do not know what to do, but our eyes are upon you"* (2 Chronicles 20:12).

Then the Scripture says, *"All the men of Judah, with their wives and children and little ones, stood there before the LORD"* (v.13).

Jehoshaphat did not know what to do, so he turned to God,

kept His eyes on God, and waited. He and the people *"stood before the Lord."* Do you know what kind of courage it takes to wait on God when a vast army is breathing down your neck? That kind of waiting requires faith. Steady and unshakable faith.

This life forces us all to wait for a million things. But the follower of Christ has the opportunity to choose joy while we are waiting on the Lord. Joy comes in the waiting if we will keep our eyes on God. Even when we don't know what to do. Even when the vast armies of this world keep approaching while we're . . . waiting.

As the story of Jehoshaphat goes, after they had been waiting, the Lord began to speak through a man named Jahaziel. Jahaziel spoke these beautiful words from God: " *'Do not be afraid or discouraged because of this vast army. For the battle is not yours, but God's. . . . You will not have to fight this battle. Take up your positions; stand firm and see the deliverance the LORD will give you'* " (v.15–17).

Jehoshaphat fell to his face and worshiped the Lord. Early the next morning, the king appointed me to go before them singing praises to God. As they sang, the Lord appointed men to set ambushes against the invading army. They were defeated. *"Then, led by Jehoshaphat, all the men of Judah and Jerusalem returned joyfully to Jerusalem, for the LORD had given them cause to rejoice"* (v.27).

We can choose joy in our waiting, assured that the outcome already belongs to the Lord. What battle are you fighting now? What enemy is breathing down your neck? Take a minute to journal your heart:

....

....

....

◎〰◎ TUESDAY ◎〰◎
YOU BELONG TO THE LORD

There are many opposing armies in our lives. Lies we believe. Difficult relationships. Financial hardships. Whatever battle you face this day, it cannot have you. You belong to God. After you have done everything you can do, then stand and wait to see the glory of God.

Where are you waiting on God today?

Pray with me today. I'll start, then you continue from your own heart:

God, I cannot see you. I have no idea what to do next. As an act of my complete trust, because I have decided to choose joy, I will stand and keep standing until you show me what to do next.

....

....

....

◎〰◎ WEDNESDAY ◎〰◎
GOD BRINGS US THROUGH THE LEAN TIMES

"*I say to myself, 'The LORD is my portion, therefore I will wait for him'* " (Lamentations 3:24).

The mature follower of Christ is learning how to joyfully wait on God. She has learned through tears, disappointment, and even rejections that sometimes it's just not her turn. That doesn't mean that it won't ever be. Or that you're not qualified. Or that you've gone completely the wrong way. It's just not yet. God decides when the waiting is over.

John Piper writes:

We are like farmers. They plow the field and plant the seed and cut away weeds and scare away crows, but they do not make the crop grow. God does. He sends rain and sunshine and brings to maturity the hidden life of the seed. We have our part. But it is not coercive or controlling. And there will be times when the crops fail. Even then God has his ways of feeding the farmer and bringing him through a lean season. We must learn to wait for the Lord.

How has God fed you through the lean seasons of your life? What is your "job" during the disappointments and battles of life?

....

....

....

THURSDAY

HOW SHALL WE WAIT?

How will we wait in joy for the Lord? Let these principles guide you:

1. *Abide.* Stay with God while you are waiting. Jesus said, "*Remain in me*" (John 15:4).

2. *Entrust* what you are waiting for into the strong hands of God: "*I know whom I have believed, and am convinced that he is able to guard what I have entrusted to him*" (2 Timothy 1:12).

3. ***Become.*** While you are waiting, actively become the person who is ready to receive what you have been waiting for.

4. ***Pray.*** Prayer is the discipline by which God gives us the ability to wait. To persevere. To trust.

5. ***Stand.*** After you have done everything that you know to do, stand and wait for the Lord.

Praying through the principles above, spend some extra time in prayer today:

....

....

....

THE WEEKEND
STAND YOUR GROUND

"*Therefore put on the full armor of God, so that when the day of evil comes, you may be able to stand your ground, and after you have done everything, to stand*" (Ephesians 6:13).

This weekend, let's take another look at yesterday's principles and answer a few of these questions:

1. Where are you with your waiting? Whining and complaining, or choosing to abide in Christ?

....

2. What do you need to do to entrust your valuable wait to God?

....

3. How can you actively become the person who is ready for God to say, "Now!"?

....

4. Are you persisting in prayer? Asking others to pray?

....

5. Your wait may require a seaSon of standing, when you don't know what else to do.

....

Wait on God and He will work, but don't wait in spiritual sulks because you cannot see an inch in front of you.

—*Oswald Chambers*

Instead of Bitterness

MONDAY

ROOT OUT BITTERNESS FROM YOUR HEART

I remember my affliction and my wandering,
the bitterness and the gall.
I well remember them,
and my soul is downcast within me.
Yet this I call to mind
and therefore I have hope:
Because of the LORD's great love we are not consumed,
for his compassions never fail.
They are new every morning;
great is your faithfulness.
—Lamentations 3:19–23

Almost every person I know has at least a hundred reasons why they could allow themselves to live in bitterness. I may have more than a hundred. Maybe you do, too. We've lived through a lot on this earth. Real-life tragedies. Awful consequences suffered. So much disappointment and heartache. I understand why bitterness comes to so many.

When we bend our heads inward and focus intently on our pain or our loss, a seed of bitterness is born inside of us. The longer and harder we focus on ourselves, the faster the root of bitterness grows. Then one day, we can't see God working all things together for good anymore. We fall into whining and complaining because we don't believe His promises are true. We cry, "Woe is me," because we can't hear His voice anymore. And besides, living as a victim actually gets some sympathy along the way.

When life catches you off guard, it's easy to give in to bitterness, wallowing in the failure and brokenness. I have certainly whined and cried and pouted at life. I have been hurt and rejected. I have been misrepresented and unheard. I'm embarrassed to tell you how easily I've given up some days. I have tasted the root of bitterness, but I have come to regard its fleeting comfort as poison.

Steve Brown writes: "Bitterness comes from our turning away from the true God. . . . Bitterness—characterized by feelings of hatred, envy, resentment, cynicism, and severity—begins when one turns from God, and it results in a disease that infects others."

It turns out that we have a choice. We do not have to allow this life to infect us with the bitter disease. You and I will become mature followers of Christ as we decide to turn back to God and choose joy instead of bitterness.

How does bitterness show up in your life? Would the people who live with you or work with you secretly say that you harbor bitterness?

....

....

....

☙ TUESDAY ❧
REMEMBER WHAT YOU BELIEVE

E very time I have allowed myself to fall into bitterness and disappointment, I realize that it's because I have listened to Satan's prompting. I have inclined my head toward his directives. I have forgotten to live what I believe. I have forgotten that God is on the throne of all creation. God's heart toward me is good. His Son is my Savior. Choosing joy over bitterness means choosing to believe that all the promises of God still hold.

Ephesians 4:30–32 asks us to *"Let all bitterness and wrath and anger and clamor and slander be put away from you, along with all malice. Be kind to one another, tender-hearted, forgiving each other, just as God in Christ also has forgiven you"* (Ephesians 4:30–32, NASB). Is there one small step you could take today to put away some of your bitterness and remember to believe God instead?

....

....

....

☙ WEDNESDAY ❧
GOD IS PLOTTING YOUR JOY

" A nd we know that in all things God works for the good of those who love him, who have been called according to his purpose" (Romans 8:28). I am certain that we have allowed bitterness to take hold of our lives because we don't really believe God. We don't believe that He is plotting for our joy. We don't believe that He is really working in all things for the good of those who love Him.

So what do you say? Let's choose the joy of believing God! Today let's begin by choosing to be free from our bitterness. Take a few minutes to process and journal about these steps to being free:

1. Confess any tendency you have toward bitterness.

2. Ask God to forgive you.

3. Turn away from the old desire to hold on to bitterness.

4. Reject Satan's lies. He doesn't want you to believe God.

5. Apply the grace of God to your circumstances. Forgive. Trust. Wait.

6. Believe God.

7. Start over every time you need to, until bitterness loses its hold.

....

....

....

THURSDAY
PUT AWAY CHILDISH THINKING

"*When I was a child, I talked like a child, I thought like a child, I reasoned like a child. When I became a man, I stopped those childish ways*" (1 Corinthians 13:11, NCV). Childish ways are for those who lack wisdom. Becoming free of our bitterness means growing up spiritually so that we are pursuing the wisdom of a mature believer, acting like a mature believer, and living in joy. Write down some ways you can resist the childish ways of bitterness and, instead, pursue the ways of joy.

....

....

....

THE WEEKEND
YOU'VE ALREADY WON!

Choosing joy instead of bitterness is mostly about continuing to believe God even when you cannot understand why. Remember that we know the end of the story. We win. The death of Jesus gives us every reason to live on this earth victorious.

1 John 5:3–5 says, "*This is the victory that conquers the world—our faith. So the one who conquers the world is the person who believes that Jesus is the Son of God*" (NCV). To choose joy over bitterness means living in the victory that has already been won. This weekend, consider and write down

three new ways you can choose to live in the victory of Jesus Christ:

1. ....

2. ....

3. ....

*Growth in wisdom may be exactly
measured by decrease in bitterness.*
—*Friedrich Nietzsche*

Serving Others

MONDAY

SERVICE BRINGS CONTAGIOUS JOY

If you have any encouragement from being united with Christ,
if any comfort from his love, if any fellowship with the Spirit,
if any tenderness and compassion, then make my **joy** *complete*
by being like-minded, having the same love, being one in spirit and purpose.
Do nothing out of selfish ambition or vain conceit,
but in humility consider others better than yourselves.
Each of you should look not only to your own interests,
but also to the interests of others.
Your attitude should be the same as that of Christ Jesus.
—Philippians 2:1–5

Last night I watched joy come home. I wish you could have been there. My husband and I stood in the church parking lot with a couple hundred other families waiting for our high school kids. They'd been away for a ten-day mission trip outside Orlando, Florida. All week, the families checked their blog and prayed for them. All week, I thought to myself, *Could it look any more miserable?*

Our 220 kids and adult chaperones spent their mission trip in living conditions that were near unbearable. The summer heat and humidity were stifling. They slept in a tent city surrounded by swarms of mosquitoes. The bathrooms were portable outdoor models. There was no kitchen, so a team of moms used gas grills to feed 220 people for the whole week. Not only were the conditions miserable, but the whole team worked incredibly hard every day to rebuild the camp that will soon house hundreds every week. My son said he's never worked so hard in his whole life.

We got to the church forty-five minutes early. This mama was ready to see her boy. As the parents waited, we eventually heard the faint sound that called us to line each side of the drive. Then we saw them: eighteen white fifteen-passenger vans, windows painted with words of encouragement, each honking its horn, the kids' hands waving. All the parents were clapping and yelling their love. I've never seen anything like it.

Then the most amazing thing happened. Two hundred and twenty of the hardest-working people I've ever met came out of their vans singing. All of them. Someone prayed and thanked God for the privilege of serving. All I could do was cry. Their joy was contagious.

It's a proven fact: if you are empty of joy, serve someone else. Serve with all of your heart. Serve for no other reason than to be like Jesus to them. In your serving, you are choosing joy.

Reflect and jot down a time in the past when you chose to serve when you felt empty:

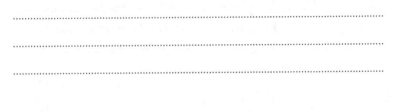

TUESDAY
FREE TO SERVE

We are not saved by serving others, but our salvation is the foundation for our service. Until we encounter God's grace, we are chained to ourselves. We're focused on our own hurts and habits. Our advantage and our goals. Galatians 5:13 says that we are *"called to be free. But do not use your freedom to indulge the sinful nature; rather, serve one another in love."* When we have been set free from our selfishness, we're free to serve. And the truth is we look most like Jesus when we are serving.

My friend, you have been set free to love others lavishly, to give as God leads you to give. Today how will you serve?

....

....

....

WEDNESDAY
THE ORDER OF THE TOWEL

"Now that I, your Lord and Teacher, have washed your feet, you also should wash one another's feet. I have set you an example that you should do as I have done for you. I tell you the truth, no servant is greater than his master, nor is a messenger greater than the one who sent him. Now that you know these things, you will be blessed if you do them" (John 13:14–17).

When I was in seminary, I met a group of men who called themselves The Order of the Towel. They took their inspiration from this passage and decided that the mark of their time together would be serving. They were great men with huge hearts of compassion, but even more they were men obviously filled with great joy.

Washing the feet of guests was the accepted practice of household servants in the culture of Jesus. Jesus stooping and tenderly washing the feet of his disciples models for us the life Christ desires us to imitate. None of us is above the lowliest servitude. You and I choose joy when we stoop, when we become willing to serve even in the most menial ways.

What is one way in the past that the Lord has asked you to stoop? How did you respond?

....

....

....

THURSDAY

NOT FOR THE FAINT OF HEART

Soak in the message of this passage in two different Bible versions: *"Nobody should seek his own good, but the good of others"* (1 Corinthians 10:24). *"We want to live well, but our foremost efforts should be to help others live well"* (1 Corinthians 10:24, The Message).

Applying the straightforward intent of this passage is not for the faint of heart. To seek the good of others consistently, faithfully, and joyfully will require a change of heart. Left to our own nature, we will pull for ourselves, plot for ourselves, and build for ourselves. But this passage is clear; we are supposed to seek the good of others.

If anyone can change our nature, it will be the Lord. Will you let the Lord change yours?

I sometimes pray this prayer: *Oh Lord, change me. I long for the joy that comes from serving. Teach me how to put others in front of myself. Help me to see them first and me second. Keep making me more and more like Jesus. Amen.*

Reflect before the Lord and write down the names of a couple of people in your life whom God is calling you to consciously put before yourself this week. Ask God for strategy in how to do this.

....

....

....

THE WEEKEND
HOW CAN I HELP?

"*Each one of us needs to look after the good of the people around us, asking ourselves, 'How can I help?'* " (Romans 15:2, The Message). This weekend, choose joy by asking this question in every setting. As you enter your workplace ask, *How can I help?* With your children or your spouse, *How can I help?* At the soccer game, *How can I help?* As you walk into church, *How can I help?*

And then maybe you turn your eyes to heaven, asking the Lord, *How can I help?*

As the weekend draws to a close, journal about what God

has shown you as you've asked this question in each setting and how that has changed your perspective.

....

....

....

I think I began learning long ago that those who are happiest are those who do the most for others.
— *Booker T. Washington*

In God's Comfort

MONDAY

TAKE YOUR ANXIETY TO THE GOD OF COMFORT

When I said, "My foot is slipping," your love, O LORD, supported me.
*When anxiety was great within me, your consolation brought **joy** to my soul.*
—Psalm 94:18–19

Cast all your anxiety on him because he cares for you.
—1 Peter 5:7

"*When anxiety was great within me.*" Oh, how many times I have lived the words of this psalm. When I became a single mom, there were years of anxiety great within me. When my dad called with the news of my mom's cancer, anxiety was great within me. A tax bill recently stirred up anxiety within me. One of my children's struggles. Being misunderstood by a friend. Maybe you are like me, and the psalmist speaks for your life, too . . . there has been anxiety great within you.

When the psalmist was consoled by the Lord, the comfort of God brought joy to his soul. The lesson seems so simple— take your anxiety to God and receive His comfort and the joy it brings! Oh how I wish I had understood this sooner. So many years of anxiousness. So much wasted worry. I finally understand that I cannot alleviate my anxiety. I cannot think it through or figure it out or hide from it or wrestle it to the ground. The only relief for my soul is the comfort that comes from God. It is His comfort that restores my joy.

The lesson of spiritual maturity becomes this: Is your soul filled with anxiety today? Run to God. Does worry taunt you in the night? Run to God. Do anxious feelings paralyze your thinking? Run to God.

It's taken me more than forty years to realize that God has put an alarm button inside my physical body. When I feel anxiety, my stomach hurts. Crazy, but goodness, why didn't I recognize it sooner? For me, stomachache means I need to take whatever concerns me to the Lord. I need His comfort. I need His strength. I need His peace. Maybe there is some kind of anxiety alarm that goes off inside of you, too. Whatever it is, heed the alarm and quickly take your anxiety to the only one who can calm your fears.

When we are filled with anxiety and emptied of joy, God will use His comfort to make an exchange in our souls. Let's begin this week with a little practice.

Close your eyes, quiet your heart and let your mind enter the presence of God. God cares for you, my friend. He is able to hold all your concerns, so in these moments, one by one, give them to Him. Name them if you can. *Lord, I give you . . .*

....

....

....

TUESDAY

THE LORD IS *YOUR* SHEPHERD

"*The LORD is my Shepherd, I shall not be in want*" (Psalm 23:1). God, who is our Shepherd, is the answer to all our anxiety. He is the great stress reliever.

The Lord is. He is a present-tense verb! He is not a *was*, or *has been*, or *will be*. The Lord *is*.

My Shepherd. He personally cares for me. Just like a shepherd tenderly cares for needy sheep, our shepherd cares for all our anxieties. He is *my* shepherd. He is *your* shepherd.

I shall not want. I can trust Him to meet all my needs. Physical. Emotional. Mental. Social. Spiritual. He is faithfully consistent. We do not have to live in want or the anxiety that comes from want.

Pray this prayer of faith, and write down a time in the past when the Lord showed you his provision:

Thank you, Lord. You are here, not somewhere far away. You are my shepherd, always attentive to my smallest concerns. You provide all that I need. May your truth be my comfort and my joy. Amen.

....

....

....

WEDNESDAY
MOVE IN CLOSER

"*Come near to God and He will come near to you*" (James 4:8). You probably already know this, but the farther we are from God, the greater the anxiousness inside of us. We begin to worry and allow our fears to increase. There is distance between us and His grace. We're off course. God's voice has grown faint.

To choose the joy of God's comfort is to move closer, lean in, and hide ourselves in Him.

Today how will you move nearer to God?

....

....

....

THURSDAY
GOD TRANSFERS HIS STRENGTH TO YOU

"*Now may our Lord Jesus Christ himself, and God our Father, who loved us and gave us eternal comfort and good hope through grace, comfort your hearts and establish them in every good work and word*" (2 Thessalonians 2:16–17, ESV). How does God give us comfort? I love the words of Hannah Whitall Smith:

We must not think of comfort in terms of "sympathy," because sympathy can weaken us instead of strengthen us. God does not pat us on the head and give us a piece of candy or a toy to distract our attention from our troubles. No, He puts strength into our hearts so we can face our trials and triumph over them.

God's comfort to us is a transfer of His strength into our souls. And in that transfer, joy is renewed. Hope is restored. New vision is given. In order to let the Lord truly comfort, you must put the full weight of your faith onto His promises.

Take just a minute to see this picture in your mind. You walk over to a sturdy chair and then confidently and comfortably sit down in the chair. You never had to give a second thought as to whether or not the chair will hold you. You knew it was strong enough.

God wants you to do the same thing with your anxiety. Put the full weight of your troubles onto Him. He is strong enough.

Pray and journal about the anxieties that you are giving to the Lord. How does it feel to be relieved of these burdens you were not asked to bear alone?

....

....

....

THE WEEKEND
SHARE THE COMFORT

"*Praise be to the God and Father of our Lord Jesus Christ, the Father of compassion and the God of all comfort, who comforts us in all our troubles, so that we can comfort those in any trouble with the comfort we ourselves have received from God*" (2 Corinthians 1:3–4). The purpose of God's comfort to us is so that we can give what we have been given. When I do not know how to give someone comfort, I begin by simply acknowledging that I see their pain. Maybe I take a loaf of bread to their house and say something like this: *I just wanted you to know I am thinking of you. My prayers are with you. I'm asking God to be your comfort right now. I'm asking Him to restore your joy.*

Where will you give God's comfort this weekend? Maybe there is someone close by who needs you to see His comfort today. Make a few notes below:

A call you could make:

....

A visit you could give:

....

A meal you could make:

....

⟪ *Never let anything so fill you with sorrow as to make you forget the joy of Christ risen.* ⟫

—*Mother Teresa*

Without Delay

MONDAY
DON'T POSTPONE JOY

*May the righteous be **glad**
and **rejoice** before God;
may they be happy and **joyful**.*
—Psalm 68:3

S itting at a stoplight a few months ago, I looked over to read this powerful three-word bumper sticker: DON'T POSTPONE JOY. Its message convicted me and impacted me at the same time. I have postponed joy too many times.

I am a doer. A planner. A logical thinker. I like creating a path that leads to somewhere I believe I am supposed to go. Because of my nature, it is very easy for me to slip into thinking of joy as a destination. A place I'm going to get to one day.

Last week, I visited an out-of-town girlfriend. We were talking with her husband about the topic of this devotional. My friend is an organized, orderly person, and her husband joked, "If order could bring you joy, then we should be the most joyous house on the street." My girlfriend confessed, "Joy is not even on the radar for me. I never even think about it. I'm just trying to survive and get through the next day. Joy seems like it's somewhere out there. Far away and unattainable."

I loved her honesty, probably because she speaks for so many of us. Joy hasn't been on our radar either. We've postponed joy until we can survive the present. We're going to experience joy once the kids are raised. Or we get that promotion. Some are waiting for joy in their retirement. Or maybe there will be joy at the next holiday or on the next vacation. It's just always some other day than today.

Another woman asked me, "How can you postpone something you've never experienced?" My heart broke for her. Some of us are postponing what we have barely tasted. Others are postponing the beginning of a pursuit. Whatever your journey with joy has been, can I encourage you this week? Do not delay any longer. Don't postpone joy. The pursuit of joy. The pleasures of joy. The peace of joy. A life filled with the joy of Christ.

So that we don't postpone joy any longer, let's spend this week learning how to pursue joy. Consider before the Lord and write down why you've been postponing joy and how the enemy may have deceived you into delay. Give these to the Lord, and ready your heart to be intentional this week.

....

....

....

TUESDAY
YOUR JOY WILL BE COMPLETE

"*Until now you have not asked for anything in my name. Ask and you will receive, and your joy will be complete*" (John 16:24). Let's specifically and boldly ask the Lord for joy, in His name:

Oh Lord, please come and fill me with the joy of my salvation. Fill me until I am overflowing. God, I long to live a joy-filled life, to radiate joy, to speak joy, to create joy for others and to bless you with every part of my life. Change me. Let my reputation become one who lives in the joy of the Lord.

God, I am choosing joy today. By the power of the Holy Spirit and in the name of your Son Jesus, will you make it so in me?

So very amen and amen.

You've asked God for joy, which is your inheritance in Christ. What strategies is the Lord giving you to live a joy-filled life?

....

....

....

WEDNESDAY
EVERY GOOD AND PERFECT GIFT

"*Every good and perfect gift is from above, coming down from the Father of the heavenly lights*" (James 1:17). Many times in my life, I have not recognized good and perfect gifts at the time. Years later I can look back and see that the delays, direction changes, and even times of loneliness were God's means to His good and perfect gifts.

I have a girlfriend who was completely surprised to become pregnant with her third son. For months during the pregnancy, she was frustrated, even angry at times. She kept telling all her friends, "I cannot believe I am pregnant. This was not supposed to happen." Today that little surprise is three years old, the delight of their family, and such a good and perfect gift.

Choose joy today by first writing down every good and perfect gift you have been given. Fill this page. Write in the margins. Use other pages if you need. Then put your hands on all the words you have written. Bow your head and bless the God who has purposed joy in your life. Thank Him for every good and perfect gift.

....

....

....

THURSDAY
FORGET YOURSELF TODAY

To choose joy today, I want you to do the most counterintuitive thing. Don't think about your joy. Try to forget yourself today. Turn anywhere that the Lord directs. Maybe you will spend this day focused on the glory of God. Maybe you will be directed to focus on your spouse or a particular child or a neighbor or friend. Maybe you are supposed to look for a stranger to care about or to open your local newspaper and let your heart be directed to care about something that has never concerned you.

Today just go crazy about somebody else. Anyone other than you. Today you are just a vessel for the love of God intended to be poured out on someone else.

Ready? Go get 'em.

THE WEEKEND

CARRY GOD'S PROMISE IN YOUR HEART

Are you ready to carry God's promise of joy in your heart? Then what about a little memory work this weekend. Memorize as many of these promises as you can:

> *Though you have not seen him, you love him; and even*
> *though you do not see him now, you believe in him and*
> *are filled with an inexpressible and glorious joy.*
> —I Peter 1:8

> *I tell you the truth, you will weep and mourn while the world*
> *rejoices. You will grieve, but your grief will turn to joy.*
> —John 16:20

> *You have made known to me the paths of life; you*
> *will fill me with joy in your presence.*
> —Acts 2:28

> *To him who is able to keep you from falling and to present you before*
> *his glorious presence without fault and with great joy—to the only*

*God our Savior be glory, majesty, power and authority, through
Jesus Christ our Lord, before all ages, now and forevermore!*
—Jude 1:24–26

ᥤ *Now and then it is good to pause in our
pursuit of joy and just be joyful.* ᥬ

—*Anonymous*

While the Storms Rage

MONDAY
HOLDING ON FOR DEAR LIFE

"Yes, indeed—God is my salvation.
I trust, I won't be afraid.
God—yes God!—is my strength and Song,
best of all, my salvation!"
Joyfully *you'll pull up buckets of water*
from the wells of salvation.
And as you do it, you'll say,
"Give thanks to God.
Call out his name.
Ask him anything!
Shout to the nations,
tell them what he's done,
spread the news of his great reputation!"
—Isaiah 12:2–4, The Message

When an awful storm blew through the southern United States in 2011, more than three hundred people lost their lives. Too many others lost their homes and all their belongings. Towns were completely devastated. Estimates to rebuild exceeded one billion dollars. The depth of sadness is immeasurable.

While most of us have seen a tornado only on news footage, many of us have been impacted by the winds of scary storms, emotionally, physically, mentally, or financially. Maybe the storm you've endured began with a phone call instead of dark clouds. Maybe it was the department layoff notice read by your manager. Maybe it was a test result the doctor grimly delivered. Though they vary, the awful devastations of life's storms have touched most of us.

The question becomes, how will we know joy in the middle of events that wound and destroy? Where in the world does joy come from in a storm?

The most awful storm I have experienced was the storm of divorce. Winds blew in from every direction; and life, as I had known it, became completely unidentifiable. My four kids and I limped through the next years together, wounded and broken. Nothing was as it had been. I know what it means to lose everything, and I also know what it means to hold on to God for dear life.

I think *holding on for dear life* is the intent of the above passage of scripture. The prophet Isaiah praises God because even when he has no strength, he does not have to be afraid, because God's strength is secure. Isaiah says that he "joyfully" draws water from the well of his salvation. The water is a spiritual water that gives comfort, protection, and peace. In the storm, there is no joy in the circumstance. Death, loss, and grief contain no joy. But like the prophet, you and I can draw joy from the well of our salvation. We can trust that God's strength will hold us and rejoice in Him.

Have you known the destruction of a storm in your life?

Maybe even today the winds of a storm are blowing all around you.

In the past, how has God renewed your joy by giving "fresh water from the well of His salvation"?

....

....

....

TUESDAY
GOD IS OUR REFUGE

Look at this passage for today: *"God is our refuge and strength, an ever-present help in trouble. Therefore we will not fear, though the earth give way and the mountains fall into the heart of the sea, though its waters roar and foam and the mountains quake with their surging. . . . The LORD Almighty is with us, the God of Jacob is our fortress"* (Psalm 46: 1–4, 7).

Every week, we continue to learn more about the manifestations of joy in the Lord. Go back through the above passage and circle the words or phrases that build a foundation for joy, even in a storm.

Now spend a few moments praying back those circled words to God as a prayer of thanksgiving; then write out some of your responses:

....

....

....

WEDNESDAY

I SHALL NOT BE MOVED

"*He only is my Rock and my Salvation; He is my Defense and my Fortress, I shall not be moved*" (Psalm 62:6, Amplified). The one who walks through a storm without the assurance of God's salvation is completely and utterly alone. He has no well from which to draw fresh water.

Maybe you have hoped something else could save you: a strong house, a good job, a happy marriage. But our salvation comes only from God. Our things and relationships on this earth are good things given to us by a good God. He means for us to enjoy His good gifts. But our soul's joy? It can come only from God.

Add your words to the following prayer:

God, I want to enjoy all that you have given to me. But I also want to live in the truth of your Scriptures. These things are blessings:

....

....

....

I thank you for every blessing, but they cannot be the source of my joy. My joy comes from you.
Amen.

THURSDAY
DRINK FROM THE WELL OF JOY

In the storms of life, our only source of joy is the well of our salvation. If you and I have depended on our circumstances for joy, we will surely fall into despair when the storms come.

Have you tried to find your joy in other ways? Maybe you have realized, like me, that other paths to joy give us only a taste of it. The life-giving, thirst-quenching joy we long for comes only from the well of God.

When we focus on our circumstances or lack, joy is fleeting, easily blown away by gale-force winds. To turn to the well for our joy means turning our focus away from the storm and back to God.

Where has your focus been?

What happens in your soul when you refocus on God?

....

....

....

THE WEEKEND
DO NOT FEAR

"*Do not fear, for I am with you; do not anxiously look about you, for I am your God. I will strengthen you, surely I will help you, surely I will uphold you with My righteous right hand*" (Isaiah 41:10, NASB). Sometime this weekend, meditate on this passage, answer the following questions, and then consider what action is required of you.

Why are you able to lay down your fear?

Answer: ....

....

Action: ....

....

What are you supposed to do with your anxiousness?

Answer: ....

....

Action: ....

....

Who will give you strength? How?

Answer: ....

....

Action: ....

....

I believe God, through His Spirit, grants us love, joy, and peace no matter what is happening in our lives. As Christians, we shouldn't expect our joy to always feel like happiness, but instead recognize joy as inner security—a safeness in our life with Christ.

—*Jill Briscoe*, Telling the Truth

When We Celebrate Believing

⟨⟩ **MONDAY** ⟨⟩

PLAN A CELEBRATION THIS WEEK

The jailer called for lights, rushed in and fell trembling before Paul and Silas.
He then brought them out and asked; "Sirs, what must I do to be saved?"
They replied, "Believe in the Lord Jesus, and you
will be saved—you and your household."
Then they spoke the word of the Lord to him
and to all the others in his house. At that hour of the night the jailer took them
and washed their wounds; then immediately he and all his family were baptized.
The jailer brought them into his house and set a meal before them;
*he was filled with **joy** because he had come to believe*
in God—he and his whole family.
—Acts 16:29–34

The jailer brings Paul and Silas into his home for a meal to celebrate! That was the decision that changed him forever. The gratefulness he felt for such a gift. His new friends. His family. A meal. And a heart full of joy. A bona fide reason for celebrating if there ever was one.

Most every weekend, I have the great privilege of explaining the word of the Lord to someone and then, as God moves in their heart, praying with them as they make the decision to believe in Jesus Christ as their Savior. When I say, "Amen," I always want to do more. That kind of decision deserves a celebration. Sometimes I jump up and down for them. Sometimes a little dance move. Many times, other people in the room erupt into applause. We all want to celebrate anytime anyone believes!

When we are apart from God, the tastes of joy that we experience are fragile and thin. Easily shattered. Quickly disappearing. To finally believe in God brings a filling of joy that is strong, glorious, and passionate. And so it seems like we ought to do a lot more celebrating!

At my house, we like to celebrate. Almost any great achievement is cause for friends, food, music, and a party. This passage makes me want to do more to celebrate new believers, renewed believers, rededicated believers.

Let's go ahead and begin looking toward the weekend. It seems obvious. There ought to be a celebration this week! A celebration of believing just for the sake of rejoicing in our salvation. Today let's begin the celebration in our hearts. Let your heart shout, "Hallelujah!" Let your soul feel the joy of having believed in the Savior. I love planning a party, and because of Christ, we couldn't have a better party to plan! So start making a few notes. Who? Where? How will you celebrate believing?

....

....

....

TUESDAY
SEND OUT INVITATIONS!

You may think I'm kidding, but I think we need a real-life celebration this week. My oldest daughter is a poor college student with lots of deadlines and things going on. So I wonder how she could work in a celebration this week. Maybe she could e-mail her friends and say,

> *Let's celebrate believing! None of us have any money, but that little fact can't stop us. Bring your own dinner to my house on Friday at 7. I'll light the candles and put on the music. We'll share a meal and laugh together. Remember to bring your gratitude. Let's celebrate belonging to God!*

No matter your circumstance, make your plans to celebrate the joy that comes from believing! Send your invitations today. Start your party list now. Who will you invite? What will the theme of your celebrations be?

....

....

....

WEDNESDAY
TESTIFY TO GOD'S WORK IN YOU

"*Come and listen, all you who fear God; let me tell you what he has done for me*" (Psalm 66:16). The celebration of believing is a way for us to tell what God has done for us. To share the fullness of joy. To testify to God's glorious work in us.

Today spend some time thinking about what God has done for you and jot down the top five things here:

1. ....

2. ....

3. ....

4. ....

5. ....

THURSDAY

SATAN DOES NOT HAVE THE LAST WORD

Henri Nouwen writes, "[We celebrate] because we see that God, not the evil one, has the last word."

No matter what your struggle today, Satan does not have the last word for the child of God. He may torment you. He may grieve you. He may trick you. But he cannot have you. You belong to God. God has the final say about your life and all that concerns you.

Take your struggles today to the Lord, and jot down the truth of what He is saying in response to the lies of the enemy.

....

....

....

@@@@@   **THE WEEKEND**   @@@@@
WE ARE ONE HAPPY PEOPLE

I love the writings of Eugene Peterson so very much. He states that God's people are those "whose lives are bordered on one side by a memory of God's acts and the other by hope in God's promises, and who along with whatever else is happening are able to say, at the center, 'We are one happy people.' "

Will you let the joy of what God has done and the hope of what He will do give your heart freedom to celebrate?

I'm hoping you have spent this week preparing to share a celebration in some creative way. May the Lord bless your time and add to your joy. As the weekend draws to a close, reflect on the celebration this week, and write down how this has affected you and your perspective.

....

....

....

A Christian should be an Alleluia from head to foot.

—*Augustine*

In the Hope of God

MONDAY

NOT WISHFUL THINKING

Be joyful in hope.
—Romans 12:12

Praise be to the God and Father of our Lord Jesus Christ!
In his great mercy he has given us new birth into a living hope
through the resurrection of Jesus Christ from the dead,
and into an inheritance that can never perish
spoil or fade—kept in heaven for you.
—I Peter 1:3–5

Hope is a confident trust in the fulfillment of something desired. Hope is also the gift of our salvation. It's the truth we cling to. We have been washed of our sins, set apart into the family of God, given the indwelling of the Holy Spirit, promised eternity in heaven. The hope of my salvation is that I am going home to my Father, and He is with me here on this earth. That's the kind of hope Paul was talking about when he instructed us to "be joyful in hope."

The hope of our salvation is not some kind of flimsy wishing. It's nothing like, "I hope I get a good grade on my paper," or "I hope they have chocolate ice cream for dessert." Our hope is a confident assurance. We are God's people. He is the king of creation. God loves us with an everlasting love. He will do all he has promised. The end.

Because we cannot earn our salvation, our hope is not dependent on our own strength or ingenuity. Because salvation is available to any who believe, anyone, from any people group to any nation, can live filled with the confident hope of God.

These hard days will try to steal your hope. Newspaper headlines. Bank-account balances. Test results. Divorce papers. Maybe yours has been stolen somewhere along the way. When our hope has been taken, joy goes, too.

May God use this week to remind us of the great hope we have been given. Because we have a living hope, let us obey the instruction of Paul and choose the joy that walks hand in hand with hope. Take some time today to reflect on the things that try to steal your hope and write a response to those things from God's Word.

....

....

....

TUESDAY
SUFFERING PRODUCES HOPE

It's embarrassing to admit that I have mostly been a coward about life. For the first forty years, I just wanted God to get me through with as little suffering as possible. If there had been an easy-breezy path, I'm sure I would have asked for that.

But life has not been easy breezy for me. Divorce. Years as a single mom. Financial struggles. Loneliness. There has been a lot. But with the hard-won vision of maturity, I can finally see that if we will persevere, suffering produces hope. And then more hope. And eventually you begin to look at everything through the eyes of hope. And, as Paul says in Romans 5:5, "*hope does not disappoint.*"

Where are you suffering today? How is your suffering producing greater hope in your spirit?

....

....

....

 **WEDNESDAY**
HOPE—THE ANCHOR OF YOUR SOUL

"*This hope we have as an anchor of the soul, a* hope *both sure and steadfast*" (Hebrews 6:19, NASB). As a young child, I remember hearing my parents talk about "the end of time." Needless to say, it scared me to death. I would go to bed trembling because I did not have the hope of Christ.

Nowadays, I am so grateful for the hope that steadies me like an anchor. Some person will stand and espouse their misled opinion about end-times or catastrophic events, and I will feel the anchor holding fast inside of me. Just last week, another prophet of doom predicted the last day of Earth and covered billboards and newspapers across this country with his prediction. I was so grateful that the hope I had inside was unwavering.

What are the fears that threaten to derail your joy? Write a response to those fears with the truth about who God is in the midst of them. Today choose the joy of being anchored by hope.

....

....

....

THURSDAY

LET HOPE SHINE

Do you know when hope shines the brightest? In the most hopeless situations. Are you up against the impossible today? Let hope shine. Have you been rejected more times than you can count? Let hope shine. Are you tired of trying? Let hope shine. Has everyone else given up and turned away? Let hope shine.

In Romans, Paul talks about Abraham and how, *"When everything was hopeless, Abraham believed anyway, deciding to live not on the basis of what he saw he couldn't do but on what God said he would do"* (4:18, The Message).

My friend, let your hope shine bright no matter how dark the circumstances. Choose the joy of hope.

Read Genesis 12:1–9, 15:1–17:27, 18:1–15, 21:1–7, and 22:1–19. Reflect on the story of Abraham and how he walked through his life despite seemingly impossible circumstances. How did he waver? How did he persevere?

....

....

....

⊙⊶⊶⊙ THE WEEKEND ⊙⊶⊶⊙
TESTIFY OF YOUR HOPE

"*But in your hearts set apart Christ as Lord. Always be prepared to give an answer to everyone who asks you to give the reason for the hope that you have*" (1 Peter 3:15). The mark of a Christian life is the presence of hope. This weekend, let someone see that mark on you. And be ready, because they will want to know where your hope comes from. As you choose the joy of hope, you will become an uncommon person in this very dark world. Be ready to tell others about your confident assurance in salvation. Be prepared to offer them the same hope you have been given.

Write down a recent testimony from your life about the faithfulness of God and the hope you have in Him; share it with whomever God brings your way this weekend. Shine, my friend, this world needs your hope.

....

....

....

⟪ *Joy and hope are never separate. I have never met a hopeful person who was depressed or a joyful person who had lost hope.* ⟫
—*Henri Nouwen*, Here and Now

When You Are Ridiculed

ᘓᕉᕉᕊᕉᕉᘐ **MONDAY** ᘓᕉᕉᕊᕉᕉᘐ

SUFFERING DISGRACE FOR THE CAUSE OF CHRIST

*The apostles left the Sanhedrin, rejoicing because
they had been counted worthy of suffering disgrace for the Name.
Day after day, in the temple courts and from house to house,
they never stopped teaching and proclaiming the
good news that Jesus is the Christ.*
—Acts 5:41–42

Bless those who persecute you; bless and do not curse.
—Romans 12:14

Today I read the most recent news from two Christian persecution websites. All over this world, Christians are being persecuted, tortured, and murdered for their faith. Today's reports were from China, India, Egypt, Iran, Pakistan, and many more areas. The websites report that just like the apostles, these Christian men and women are choosing joy in the face of horrendous consequences. I have no personal experience with the kind of persecution my brothers and sisters are facing, yet their faithfulness inspires me.

I am ridiculed only occasionally. Snubbed sometimes. Misunderstood. Surely I can choose joy when I am left out because of my faith, when I am joked about for my obedience. The persecution I have experienced is more of a mockery, wounding only to the spirit—nothing like that of the people I just prayed for who are suffering in prisons around the world.

Maybe the persecution you have faced has been a form of ridicule, too. An exclusion. A loneliness. The question for us becomes, will we choose the joy of the apostles when we suffer disgrace for the cause of Christ?

How can we turn this around so that the wounded spirit of rejection becomes joy for the sake of our Lord? Several times I have had the opportunity to share my faith on an airplane. The conversation usually begins with a seatmate asking what I do. Sometimes, that question strikes up a beautiful conversation or a sweet time of fellowship. But occasionally, my response about my faith has abruptly ended all hopes of a conversation. There is a swift rejection and several more hours of awkward silence, seat belt to seat belt.

I have learned to rejoice in the awkwardness and even in the rejection. Hallelujah that I had the opportunity to clearly say the truth of Jesus. Praise God that that person talked to a woman who is earnestly seeking God instead of some nutcase who misrepresents the simplicity of the gospel. Even when I have been rejected or ridiculed, there is a joy that springs up inside of me because I have been obedient to testify about my faith.

This week, let us choose joy, even if it means we will be ridiculed or, worse, persecuted. May the ridicule you endure increase your joy and strengthen your resolve to live for Christ.

Can you remember the last time someone mocked your faith? How did it make you feel?

....

....

....

TUESDAY
GOD'S POWER WHEN WE ENDURE

"The Message that points to Christ on the Cross seems like sheer silliness to those hellbent on destruction, but for those on the way of salvation it makes perfect sense. This is the way God works, and most powerfully as it turns out" (1 Corinthians 1:18, The Message). The truth is, some people just aren't going to get it. They won't get your joy and they won't understand your faith. They will try to make a mockery of you. Belittle you. Wound you.

I think of the mom whose teenage child rejects her faith. The cross seems silly to the child on the path of destruction. Sweet mama, hang in there with your wayward child. Forgive him or her. Pray for your child. Do not let your child's persecution or their teasing steal your joy.

It turns out that God works powerfully when we endure. Stand underneath the pressure. Write out a prayer of endurance and forgiveness, specifically seeking God's purposes and clarity for the ones who have mocked your faith.

....

....

....

WEDNESDAY
GLADLY TAKING THE MOCKING

My kids go to Christian schools. They have Christian friends. They participate in all kinds of Christian activities. And yet, even in those circles, each one of them has encountered persecution.

A few weeks ago, my teenage son's voice began to quiver when he told me about a sleepover with some Christian friends. Evidently, a couple of the guys began to talk about girls in less-than-flattering ways. My son worked up his courage and said he didn't want to talk like that. With that quivering voice he told me, "Mom, they looked at me like I was an alien. It was awful."

Maybe you've felt like an alien in your circle, too. I sure have. But it's going to happen. 2 Timothy 3:12 says that *"all who desire to live a godly life in Christ Jesus will be persecuted"* (ESV). May we learn to regard even that kind of persecution with a deep and comforting joy.

Mocked for choosing godliness. I'll take it.

Have you ever felt completely out of place because of your commitment to godliness? How did the Lord strengthen you in that time?

....

....

....

❧ THURSDAY ❧
HOLD TO GOD'S TRUTH

"*If you are insulted because of the name of Christ, you are blessed, for the Spirit of glory and of God rests on you*" (1 Peter 4:14). God's truth is not always convenient or comfortable but it is always the truth. We are charged with giving and living in truth. Then if we are insulted, so be it. Receive the blessing of knowing God's Spirit rests on you. Live in the joy of knowing that you are living in obedience and God is your covering.

Consider a time when God's truth was not comfortable. How did you handle the situation? What were the consequences?

....

....

....

❧ THE WEEKEND ❧
LOOK TO HEAVEN FOR APPROVAL

In order to choose joy when we are ridiculed or even persecuted, a shift has to be made. We must shift our need for approval from earth to heaven. So before your next encounter, make these three decisions and write out each of these verses:

1. Decide to please God before men (see Galatians 1:10):

....

2. Fear God, not man (see Matthew 10:33):

....

3. And no matter what comes, don't be ashamed of Christ
   (see Mark 8:38):

....

*⟪ Joy is not what we have to acquire in order
to experience life in Christ; it is what comes to
us when we are walking in the way of faith and
obedience. ⟫*

—*Eugene Peterson,* Perseverance

WEEK 39

....

In Abiding

CHRIST'S PARTING MESSAGE—ABIDE

As the Father has loved me, so have I loved you.
Abide in my love. If you keep my commandments, you will abide in my love,
just as I have kept my Father's commandments and abide in his love.
*These things I have spoken to you, that my **joy** may be in you,*
*and that your **joy** may be full.*
—John 15:9–11, ESV

O n the very night He would be betrayed by Judas, Jesus
took his disciples to an upstairs room to be with them
for an evening. Jesus knew this was his last night with them.
He knew that later, in an olive grove, Judas would betray him,
soldiers would arrest him, and ultimately, the cross would be
His fate.

What do you tell someone just before you leave them?
You tell them the most important things. His words that night
have become known as the Upper Room Discourse. They are
four powerful chapters, spoken to the disciples around a table
and still speaking to us this very day.

Jesus wanted the disciples to know how to live when he was not physically with them. Eleven times in ten verses, he says, "Abide in me." *Abide* means "stay." Remain. Don't go anywhere. Don't wander off. No matter what comes, stay with me. No matter how dark, stay with me.

Jesus gives that same instruction to us, and then He clearly states His purpose: so that my joy may be in you and that your joy may be full. We are to abide in Christ so that we will be full of joy.

This week, we will walk through this passage together. Each day, let's practice the discipline of abiding in Christ. Being with Him. Hiding ourselves in His presence. As we choose to faithfully abide in Him, we will be choosing joy.

Write out a prayer committing this week to practicing what it is to abide in Christ.

....

....

....

TUESDAY
THE JOY OF BEING A BRANCH

"*I am the true vine, and my Father is the gardener. . . . I am the vine; you are the branches*'" (John 15:1, 5). In the first verses of John 15, our Lord describes a new relationship between Himself and His followers. He is the true vine, believers are the branches, and the Father is the vine-keeper.

I love being a branch. My only job is to remain connected to the vine. Jesus, as the vine, is the source of nourishment. He

gives me life and feeds me daily. The Father is the vine-keeper.
I am protected and guided by His care.

Abiding is our obligation. Producing fruit is God's concern. We have the great privilege of seeking the fellowship of
Jesus and leaving the fruit to Him.

Today you are a branch. All you have to do is remain connected to the vine. Stay with Him. Abide in His presence. Let
Jesus take care of the rest.

Make a list of the concerns and worries you've been carrying that are not your burdens to bear. Then release those to
the Lord and focus on being in His presence.

....

....

....

WEDNESDAY
PRACTICE ABIDING

What fruit will we produce when we abide in Christ?
Spiritual fruit. Everlasting fruit. Fruit that will feed
others in the family of God. Fruit that will be glorifying to
God. Abiding is believing, depending, and persevering until
there is fruit.

We will not produce spiritual fruit in our lives because we
have read a new book or attended a great conference. We will
bear fruit only because we have remained in Christ. In John
15:4–5, Jesus says, *"As the branch cannot bear fruit by itself, unless
it abides in the vine, neither can you, unless you abide in me . . . apart
from me you can do nothing"* (ESV). Pursuing intimacy. Keeping

a conversation with Him through prayer. Learning His ways through His word. Apart from God, we will have nothing.

How will you practice abiding in Christ today?

....

....

....

THURSDAY
PRODUCING SPIRITUAL FRUIT

"*If a man remains in me and I in him, he will bear much fruit*" (John 15:5). We looked at the progression of this passage before. When we stay with Jesus, our lives begin to produce spiritual fruit. When we keep on staying with Him, we bear much fruit. There is great reward for those who persevere in the faith. Those who resolve to keep themselves connected to Jesus no matter what comes.

I long for that progression in my own life! I'm praying that year after year of faithfulness to Jesus will begin to bear much spiritual fruit in my life. I want my husband to enjoy being married to a spiritual woman. I want my children to benefit from the fruit God is producing in my life. I desire my life to become the testimony of a broken woman holding on to Jesus for dear life. He promises fruit for a life like that.

What kind of fruit do you desire in your own life as a result of remaining in Him?

....

....

....

THE WEEKEND
TRUST AND OBEY

"*By this my Father is glorified, that you bear much fruit and so prove to be my disciples. As the Father has loved me, so have I loved you. Abide in my love. . . . These things I have spoken to you, that my joy may be in you, and that your joy may be full*" (John 15:8–9,11 ESV). I want to encourage you. There are no special techniques or formulas for abiding in Christ. In its simplest form, abiding is trusting the Lord and obeying His word. Abiding is keeping yourself in a life-giving relationship with Jesus. It is the only way to fruitfulness.

If I want all the joy that God has ordained for me on this earth—and my friend, I really do!—then it will be attained as I practice the discipline of abiding. Staying. Remaining in Christ.

This weekend, would you set apart a little extra time for the Lord? A little more quiet in His presence? A longer time in prayer? Let the true vine strengthen you. Let His word feed you. All you need to do is be with Him. He will take care of the growth.

Reflect and write about what God speaks to you in your extra time with Him this weekend.

....

....

....

The joy we can't produce and the world can't take away is the joy He imputes by His Spirit.
—Lloyd John Ogilvie

In Our Trials

MONDAY
A SERIOUS PURSUIT

*Consider it pure joy, my brothers, whenever you face trials of many kinds,
because you know that the testing of your faith develops perseverance.
Perseverance must finish its work so that you may be
mature and complete, not lacking anything.*
—James 1:2–4

I have been avoiding this famous James passage about joy.
When I began this book, I knew that I'd have to get here,
but obviously, I've been dragging my feet. When people hear
that you are writing a devotional about joy, I think they assume
you're writing about the fluffy-cloud kind of joy. You know, *I'm
choosing joy at the yogurt shop, with extra sprinkles! Choosing joy
under a beach umbrella with your warm toes in the sand.*

But the Bible has yet to offer up one passage about light-
n-fluffy, cherry-on-top, easy-breezy joy. As a matter of fact, the
joy of the Scriptures is a serious pursuit for those who long to
become spiritually mature. To choose joy is a Christlike endeavor and a willing act of obedience to God. To remain a joy-

less Christian is disobedience. In all things, no matter what comes, the character of a Christian is to be marked by joy.

And now we come to the first verse of the weighty passage above: *"Consider it pure joy, my brothers, whenever you face trials of many kinds."* Since this is such a pivotal joy passage, I'd like to take this week and camp on its importance.

Let's begin with the very first word, *"consider."* To consider means that we have a choice about how we will view our trials. We can take the natural view and see our trials as punishment, harboring resentment, bitterness, and anger. Or we can choose to think supernaturally, from God's vantage point, seeing our trials with spiritual eyes.

To consider means to think it through and then respond with thoughtfulness. It's so much easier to react first than to take a moment to think. To ask yourself questions like, *Am I alone or is God in control? Will I react based on my feelings or respond to this trial with obedience?*

When faced with trials, the first thing James asks us to do is stop for a moment to consider.

Today take a moment to consider before you react. Will you respond in the supernatural, choosing the joy that God provides to you? Or will you react in your humanity, based on your feelings?

....

....

....

TUESDAY

PURE JOY

"*Consider it pure joy*" (James 1:2). This is amazing to me. God wants us to view our trials with an attitude of joy. They are not to be viewed as a punishment, a curse, or a calamity but as something that should prompt rejoicing, for goodness sake! And the passage is clear: trials are to produce a pure joy in us, not just a trace of joy mixed with fear and frustration. Pure joy is what the Lord requires.

And by the way, this kind of pure joy is not to be misunderstood as pretending. No one is supposed to pretend anything. We are to allow the supernatural indwelling of God's Holy Spirit to transform our minds so that we consider our trials with pure joy.

Is this truth rocking your world? It sure is mine! James has not stuttered. We have understood him correctly. Pure joy in the face of our trials means all, not part, but the whole of us filled with joy.

Write a prayer today, putting aside any pretending and fear and asking God to plant in your heart an attitude of pure joy.

....

....

....

WEDNESDAY
JOY IN THE MIDDLE OF TRIALS

"*Whenever you face trials of many kinds*" (James 1:2). Most of us prefer to consider it pure joy when we escape our trials. James wants us to choose pure joy right in the middle of them. All kinds of them. This morning I had a little trial with one of my children. My mom is currently facing a different kind of trial in chemotherapy. In Greek, the wording of this passage is clear that these kinds of trials are external trials or tests of stamina that each one of us will encounter in all kinds of ways during a lifetime.

We also have to pay attention to James's choice of words. He did not say "if," he said "when." The trials are coming, and for many of us, today has already been full of them.

Inside the various trials that will come your way today—when they come, not if—will you choose to rejoice?

....

....

....

THURSDAY
REFINED BY FIRE

"*Because you know that the testing of your faith develops perseverance*" (James 1:3).

"*In this you greatly rejoice, though now for a little while you may have had to suffer grief in all kind of trials. These have come so that your faith—of greater worth than gold, which perishes even though refined by fire—may be proved genuine and may result in praise, glory and honor when Jesus Christ is revealed"* (1 Peter 1:6–7).

The reason we choose joy in our trials is because a valuable reward is being produced in us. True faith yields perseverance. And perseverance means steadfastness in the face of difficulty. Faith in the face of trials is like gold, it stands the tests of fire!

James wants us to understand that choosing joy in our trials is flexing our faith muscle. Making it stronger. Developing our character and our ability to persevere.

Honestly, I am a fire avoider. I don't naturally run toward trials and difficulty. But the Bible says we can't avoid everything. There will be trials. You and I will be right in the middle of them. And in that fire, choosing joy will produce a faith that is like gold!

Think of a time in the past when choosing joy in the midst of a trial yielded great things, and write about it, remembering God's faithfulness to work good in all things.

....

....

....

THE WEEKEND
THE GOAL—SPIRITUAL MATURITY

"Perseverance must finish its work so that you may be mature and complete, not lacking anything" (James 1:4). It turns out that choosing joy in our trials has one main goal: spiritual maturity. God wants us to be mature and complete, not lacking in anything.

With spiritual maturity as the goal, we must choose joy whenever we face trials of any kind.

This weekend, how will you begin to choose joy in the small and the great trials in your life?

....

....

....

Why does God allow some of His deeply loved sons and daughters to go through trials of body and spirit? Because, if they receive that suffering with faith and joy, that supernatural chemical reaction will supercharge the message of His Son's love and the suffering one will have the privilege of a life impact that will keep echoing and echoing beyond their years.

—*Joni Eareckson Tada,* A Lifetime of Wisdom: Embracing the Way God Heals You

In Generosity

GENEROSITY LEARNED THROUGH LOSS

They are being tested by many troubles, and they are very poor.
*But they are also filled with abundant **joy**,*
which has overflowed in rich generosity.
—2 Corinthians 8:2, NLT

I wish I'd known sooner what generosity does for your soul. I've been a stingy old bird. Even as a teenager, I kept things for myself. The last piece of cake. My class notes I didn't want anyone else to have. Goofy things, but such a sad indication of the condition of my soul. I was selfish. Through the years, I didn't acquire new things to hoard; I just hoarded what I had. In case I might need it one day. My hoard was neat, labeled, and organized. Ridiculous.

But thank the Lord, God did not leave me that way. In my divorce, the kids and I lost almost everything. There is something about losing everything that teaches you about the generosity of God. Somewhere in those years of nothing, by the power of the Holy Spirit, God changed me. God pried my hands open to take away everything, but through the lesson of losing, He taught me to leave my hands open, allowing Him to move things in and out of my life. Placing them where they serve Him best.

In our leanest years, God moved in the hearts of family and friends to share so much. When I was a single mom, many people were generous beyond reasonableness with their time, energies, money, and things. Neighbors went out of their way to help me with my children. Friends willingly gave me things we needed for our home. My parents sacrificed to be there for the children and me.

I learned so much from the people who lavished us with their generosity. First, they listened to God and responded quickly. They didn't wait a couple of weeks to see if they still felt like helping. People just jumped in where there was a need, many times forsaking their own comfort or something they could have had for themselves.

And second, I watched their joy increase. Turns out that generosity multiplies joy like a holy fertilizer. Once you get a taste of that kind of joy, you're hooked. Generosity grows joy in the soul!

I didn't know it at the time, but losing everything was one of the best things that ever happened to me. And now the great lesson of giving generously has become mine to multiply for God's glory. I know that God wants me to return what was done for me.

Have you ever lost everything? Been down on your luck? How did the generosity of others affect you?

....

....

....

TUESDAY
GIVING CAN BE ADDICTIVE—IN A GOOD WAY!

" *Give away your life; you'll find life given back, but not merely given back—given back with bonus and blessing. Giving, not getting, is the way. Generosity begets generosity*" (Luke 6:38, The Message). Once you get the hang of it, giving can become addictive! There is such a real and instantaneous joy produced in the soul that you just want to keep going back for more!

Quick, how can you be generous today? With your time? Your energy? Even with some of your money? Try to choose something intentional before the day is through. Spend a few moments asking God to direct you and get ready for the sweet infusion of joy that comes with your giving!

....

....

....

WEDNESDAY
QUICK! DO SOMETHING GOOD

In this world, people teach you to hold your cards close. Don't let anyone else know your tricks. Don't give away your contacts or share your helpful relationships. Don't show someone else the way, stay in front of them.

Proverbs 3:27 flies directly in the face of that teaching: "*Do not withhold good from those who deserve it, when it is in your power to act.*" We're supposed to help one another. We cannot withhold good from someone who deserves it. For me, that might mean introducing a new author to my publisher. Or promoting someone else's work above mine. Or cheering loudly for my friends who are farther down the road or financially more successful.

When it is in your power to act, do not delay. Quickly do good for all who deserve it. Who is someone you can help today? In what way can you share what God has blessed you with?

....

....

....

༄ THURSDAY ༄
CHOOSE THE BLESSING OF GIVING

Last weekend I spoke at a women's event. After the conference, my sweet hostess gave me a beautiful, unique handmade bracelet as a gift. I loved that bracelet and probably wore it every day after she had given it to me. A few days ago, my twenty-one-year-old daughter spotted it, wanted to try it on, said she really liked it, and handed it back to me. The old me would have put that thing right back on my arm. The new me didn't want to miss the blessing. It was joy for me to give it to my daughter, even more than when I first received the gift.

Paul knew this kind of joy in Acts 20:35, when he spoke to the Ephesians: " *'In everything I did, I showed you that by this kind of hard work we must help the weak, remembering the words the Lord Jesus himself said: "It is more blessed to give than to receive."' "*

Choose the blessing today. Choose the joy. Give.

Is there something God is calling you to give today? Have you been holding anything back and thereby robbing yourself of the blessing?

....

....

....

THE WEEKEND
LAVISH GIVING

A few years ago, God introduced me to the work of World Vision and the ministry of child sponsorships all around the world. I have traveled with their ministry and seen with my own eyes the powerful difference their work is making.

Their work is funded by generosity. People who choose the joy of giving so that someone else can be helped. My family sponsors six children in three different countries in Africa. And I tell you, when the Lord blesses, we're going to sponsor an entire village!

I am absolutely sure that God has entrusted me with financial blessings so that I can give. And now that He has unclenched my greedy hands, my husband and I have decided that we want all the rest of our years on the earth to be about giving lavishly and generously.

Sure, we get the joy, but in our obedience, God gets the glory!

This weekend, look around. Don't wait for your hands to be pried open. Begin to give and look for more opportunities to live generously. In your giving, God will fill you with joy, multiplied joy. More joy than you believed you had the capacity to hold. As the weekend draws to a close, write about the opportunities God showed you and what came of them.

....

....

....

❧ Really big people are, above everything else, courteous, considerate, and generous—not just to some people in some circumstances—but to everyone all the time. ❧

—*Thomas J. Watson, Sr.*

WEEK 42

JOY

In Gratitude

With joy you will draw water from the wells of salvation.
—Isaiah 12:3

If ever there was a lesson moms the world over are trying to teach their children, it's the lesson of gratefulness and gratitude. I still catch myself whispering to my teenage children, "Say thank you." Nudging their self-centered hearts to move a little. Trying to plant a few more seeds of thankfulness. Some days, downright forcing them to write a thank-you note or make a call to tell someone thanks.

But sadly, saying thank-you, even if you really mean it, does not fully embrace all that gratitude should be. Gratitude is more than a few words or a handwritten note or delighting over a gift you wanted to receive. John Piper says, "Gratitude is the feeling of happiness you feel toward somebody who has shown you some undeserved kindness, that is, who has been gracious to you."[1]

Gratitude finds its source in our salvation. The one who has believed in Christ has been given a deep well of gifts through salvation. It is with joy that we draw the water of gratitude for all we have been given.

Gratitude for our salvation is more than just an occasional thank-you to God or a praise song on Sunday morning. This kind of gratitude is a genuine feeling of joy you have toward God for the undeserved kindness and grace He has given to you.

You and I are called to live in the joy of gratitude. It's become a trendy idea to keep a gratitude journal. I think that it's a really great idea to write down what you're grateful for. So today take some time to be specific and journal your own gratitude to God for your salvation.

....

....

....

TUESDAY
WALK IN GRATEFULNESS

"*So then, just as you received Christ Jesus as Lord, continue to live in him, rooted and built up in him, strengthened in the faith as you were taught, and overflowing with thankfulness*" (Colossians 2:6–7). We are supposed to overflow with thankfulness for our salvation. *Overflow* means "spilling, streaming, flooding." Our gratefulness is supposed to spill over. When we walk into a room, we're supposed to be dripping gratefulness. With every encounter and person we meet, gratefulness should slosh out.

How do you walk into a room? What would it look like for you to walk in grateful?

....

....

....

WEDNESDAY
GOD'S GOOD GIFTS

On Monday, you wrote your gratitude for your salvation. Today let's give thanks to God for His good gifts. Psalm 107:1 reminds us to *"Give thanks to the LORD, for he is good; his love endures forever."* Jot your blessings below. Count them if you can.

....

....

....

THURSDAY
THE CHARACTER OF GRATITUDE

Someone has said that you can overcome grumbling with gratitude. I do believe that choosing the joy of gratitude will change you. Maybe you need an attitude of gratitude. Maybe you've spent enough years fussing and fuming. Paul says that as Christians, we should be *"Giving thanks always and for everything to God the Father in the name of our Lord Jesus Christ"* (Ephesians 5:20, ESV).

Do you know a grateful person? Some characteristics of grateful people are humility, contentment, acceptance, supportiveness. What are the characteristics of gratitude you most desire?

....

....

....

Now turn those desires into prayers.

⊙ಿ⊱⊰ಿ⊚ THE WEEKEND ⊙ಿ⊱⊰ಿ⊚
BRIMMING WITH WORSHIP

They say you will become what you think about most. In order for us to become grateful people, living in the joy of gratitude, we will have to change our thinking. Redirect our thinking.

When we stop thinking about the wonderful gifts of our salvation, our spiritual fire goes out. We forget to live in gratefulness. Psalm 100:2–4 reminds us to *"Know that the LORD is God. It is he who made us, and we are his; we are his people, the sheep of his pasture. Enter his gates with thanksgiving and his courts with praise; give thanks to him and praise his name."* Maybe you'll need to look at your gratitude lists often until your mind remembers more quickly to be thankful. Maybe you will need to meditate consistently on the rich treasures you have in God. I love this promise from Isaiah 26:3: *"You keep him in perfect peace whose mind is stayed on you"* (ESV).

And this exhortation from Hebrews 12:28: *"Do you see what we've got? An unshakable kingdom! And do you see how thankful we must be? Not only thankful, but brimming with worship, deeply reverent before God"* (The Message).

This weekend, let's see what we've got and live gratefully, brimming with worship for our God. Reflect on all that God has blessed you with, and write down three specific things you will focus on and remember throughout the weekend, redirecting your mind.

....

....

....

❧ Gratitude can transform common days into thanksgivings, turn routine jobs into joy, and change ordinary opportunities into blessings. ❧
—*William Arthur Ward*

In Faithful Work

STEP INTO YOUR MASTER'S JOY

His master said to him, "Well done, good and faithful servant.
You have been faithful over a little; I will set you over much.
*Enter into the **joy** of your master."*
—Matthew 25:21, ESV

In the Parable of the Talents, three men are given talents (a measure of money) by a man going on a journey. The first man gets five. The second gets two. The last man gets one. Jesus says that each was given talents according to his abilities. When the man returns from his journey, the first man has multiplied the talents and gives his master the original five plus five more. The second man has done the same and returns his two plus two more. The master responds to them both: *"Well done, good and faithful servant. You have been faithful over a little; I will set you over much. Enter into the joy of your master."*

The last man comes to his master and returns his original talent. He has not multiplied his one into one more. Instead, he dug a hole and hid his talent until the master returned.

The master is furious with the last man and orders him to be thrown outside, into the darkness.

I think about this parable a lot. Most of the time I feel like I have been entrusted with five talents. I am the daughter of godly people. I received a wonderful education. God has blessed me with opportunities, and I want to be faithful with the work He has entrusted to me. I long to step into my master's joy.

I also think a lot about the man who dug the hole. The Bible says he was afraid. I understand those fears. It's the play-it-safe-and-dig-a-hole fear. Afraid of failing. Afraid of being laughed at. Afraid of losing the one talent he had been given. I imagine that he, too, longed for his master's joy, but he allowed his fears, maybe even his laziness, to disqualify him.

When we choose to pursue the joy of faithful work, we are choosing the way of God's favor and blessing.

I long to hear my Father say, "Well done." Well done, daughter. Well done, wife. Well done, Mama. Well done, Bible teacher. Well done, neighbor. Well done, servant.

Just the anticipation of His joy brings tears to my eyes. And renews my commitment. I want to be faithful in the work God has given to me.

This week, we will talk about choosing the joy of faithful work. Let's begin with one question: what talents have been entrusted to you?

....

....

....

TUESDAY
THE JOY OF WORK

"*All hard work brings a profit, but mere talk leads only to poverty*" (Proverbs 14:23). The thing about hard work is that it's just so daily! Day after day, month after month. Persistence is required. Faithfulness is needed. We get up and begin the whole thing over again.

I know a man who just decided to stop working. He'd had enough and had plenty of money. But the years have gone by and he has spent his time talking, and just like the proverb, the man lives near poverty.

We must choose the joy of faithful work, or two things will happen. Poverty will be our fate. We will not be invited into our Master's joy.

Today let's work hard. Let's use our minds for the glory of God. Create with our hands for His renown. Serve other people so that we will be like Him. Have you been talking more than you have been working hard? In what areas of your life is God calling you to be more diligent?

....

....

....

WEDNESDAY
LAZINESS IS THE ENEMY OF FAITHFUL WORK

"*A little sleep, a little slumber, a little folding of the hands to rest—and poverty will come on you like a bandit and scarcity like an armed man"* (Proverbs 24:33–34). Laziness is the enemy of faithful work. And oh my goodness, will this world lure you in. There is a time for rest. A time for play. A time for restoration. We'd do well to examine our lives to see if we have stepped over into any areas of laziness.

Start your prayer with the following and finish it more personally, writing down the rest of your prayer:

Father, show me where I have become lazy. Remove that inclination. Retrain my mind. Forgive me for sinning against you. Lord, strengthen me for faithful work and the joy you have promised!

....

....

....

THURSDAY

TAKE JOY IN THE TALENTS YOU'RE GIVEN

When the master gave the talents, he gave according to their abilities. He assigned each one a different work, based on His knowledge of their gifts, their capacity, their means, etc. To this very day, God gives our assignments based on His intimate knowledge of what He has prepared us to do.

We choose joy when we are faithful to do the work God has assigned to us. It won't do us any good to strive for someone else's talents or assignment. We have been given ours. Galatians 6:4 says, *"Each one should test his own actions. Then he can take pride in himself, without comparing himself to somebody else."* We should test ourselves before the Lord and ask Him, "Am I on task? Am I being faithful to do what you wanted me to do?"

Too often we are looking around, making unfair comparisons, measuring ourselves by someone else's talent.

My friend, choose the joy of being faithful to the work God has given to *you*. What is that work specifically and strategically assigned to you? Have you been on task?

....

....

....

THE WEEKEND
DIG UP YOUR BURIED TALENT

Got a talent buried in the backyard? This weekend would be a great time to dig it up. Go ahead. Time's a wasting. The Master has great plans for all He has entrusted to you. So grab a shovel and dig!

Ask the Lord to show you what tasks He has entrusted to your care. Have you been held back by fear? What steps can you take this weekend to remedy that?

....

....

....

Opportunity is missed by most because it is dressed in overalls and looks like work.
—*Thomas Alva Edison*

WEEK 44

In Friendship and Hospitality

CHOOSE THE JOY OF FRIENDSHIP

They worshiped together at the Temple each day,
met in homes for the Lord's Supper,
*and shared their meals with great **joy** and generosity.*
—Acts 2:46, NLT

I used to be a really good friend to people, but more recently, like in the past twenty years, I have been a friendship failure. Well, maybe not a total failure, but pretty close. I have blamed it on my kids, all four of them. I adore them, and their lives consume me. And the single-mom years. And working to provide. And ministry. And falling in love with my beautiful husband. The last twenty years have been busy, and I have not been the friend I intended to be.

Just for the record and the sake of confession, I made promises I did not keep. I lost touch with people I really love. I have not returned every call, e-mail, text, Tweet, or post that has been sent to me. I have missed out on the places you re-connect, like reunions and homecomings and parties and such. I have not celebrated the friends I adore with all the love I have for them. I have not made the effort. And ultimately, I have missed out on joy.

There was an article online this morning that reported people in my age group (45–64) are currently the unhealthi-est and saddest of all the ages. And I can tell you why. We are in-over-our-heads busy, praying our kids through adolescence, paying our mortgages, building our retirement funds, and trying to get something on the table for dinner every night. When other people catch a glimpse of my family's calendar, they faint or at least gasp for breath and hold their chests.

But I cannot let this pattern continue. I am missing the sweetest kind of joy that comes from pursuing friendships and hospitality.

This week is written mostly for me, but oh how I pray God will minister to you and encourage you through this. Let us choose the joy of togetherness, shared journeys, and friend-ship in the body of Christ.

How is it with you and friendships? Are you nurturing one friend well or have you been like me, out of action for too many years now?

....

....

....

❦ TUESDAY ❦
FRIENDS LOVE THROUGH ALL KINDS OF WEATHER

I love this story:

Although the North American Indians had no written alphabet before they met the white man, their language was anything but primitive. The vocabulary of many Indian nations was as large as that of their French and English exploiters, and often far more eloquent. Compare the coldness of "friend" with "one-who-carries-my-sorrows-on-his-back." [1]

So many friends and family members have been just this for me; they have carried my sorrows on their backs. They have been the friends mentioned in Proverbs, who *"love through all kinds of weather"* (17:17, The Message). Now it's time for me to choose the joy of becoming that kind of friend again. The kind who jumps in and stands under a heavy load. The kind who walks alongside you on the difficult road.

Is there a friend who needs your back for their sorrows? May we both choose the joy of jumping in.

....

....

....

❦ WEDNESDAY ❦
BE A FRIEND WHO "LEANS IN"

I'm sure you've read this somewhere: a friend is one who comes in when the whole world has gone out.

John 15:13 says, " *'This is the very best way to love. Put your life on the line for your friends'* " (The Message). A friend will put her reputation on the line to stand beside you. She will believe in you when all has seemed to fail. She will plant flowers in your yard because she thinks you need them. She will show up in court to hold your hand. She will mop your floor because you don't have time. She will fold your load of towels because the dryer beeped.

The very best kind of friend moves closer when everyone else runs away. She gets closer. Stays longer. Holds you tighter.

I choose the joy of becoming the kind of friend who leans in. What small ways can you lean in to a friend this week?

....

....

....

THURSDAY
UNGRUDGING HOSPITALITY

" *Above all hold unfailing your love for one another, since love covers a multitude of sins. Practice hospitality ungrudgingly to one another*" (1 Peter 4:8–9, RSV). Ungrudgingly. That means we should be the kind of people who like to practice hospitality! Choosing the *joy* of hospitality, not the burden. When we practice the discipline of hospitality, we receive the joy of being God's instrument of grace and refreshment.

Like the early church, let us commit to inviting people to meet together in our homes, where we share meals with great joy and generosity. Who is God putting in your heart to invite into your home this week? Send an invitation today.

....

....

....

THE WEEKEND
ENTERTAINING ANGELS

"*Do not forget to entertain strangers, for by so doing some people have entertained angels without knowing it*" (Hebrews 13:2). Well, alrighty then. We have officially been put on angel alert. Evidently they may want to come to your house this weekend. Consider a few ideas to get yourself ready to entertain, just in case an angel does decide to drop by.

Do not wait to invite people over until you have new carpeting or plates that match. They have old carpeting and mismatched plates, too.

Make entertaining easy on yourself. A potluck every time is fine. Sharing is such a blessing to everyone.

Focus more on the heart than on the food. Let the dishes stack up and visit.

Be intentional about building the disciplines of hospitality and friendship into your life.

....

....

....

Wishing to be friends is quick work,
but friendship is a slow-ripening fruit.
—*Aristotle*

WEEK 45

JOY

In the Mundane

MONDAY
RELISH THE ORDINARY

*Be glad in the LORD and **rejoice**, you righteous ones;*
*And shout for **joy**, all you who are upright in heart.*
—Psalm 32:11, NASB

Rejoice** in the Lord always. I will say it again: **Rejoice!
—Philippians 4:4

I like to think that I have a pretty great life. Coolest job ever. A Savior to serve. A family and husband whom I adore. A love of travel and lots of it to do. Yep, I really do have a great life, with lots of highlights and fun opportunities.

But the truth is the high spots are just that: spots. Fun blips on my life's map. The great majority of my time is spent in the mundane and the unexciting. You know mundane; it's the stuff that holds the rest of our life together. It's the little things that have to be done. The routine. The monotonous. And many days, the downright boring.

Most of my days begin the same way with the alarm going off at 6:30 a.m. I patter to the kids' rooms and wake them for school. Then go back to my son's room to wake him twice more. The whirlwind before school is the same routine every day. There is a flurry of eating, gathering homework, barking dogs, and tracking down the wayward sports clothes. When they're all out the door, I read the front page of the newspaper, begin a load of laundry, decide if I'm wearing make-up that day or not, then shuffle to my computer to begin the e-mail sorting and to-do list making. Mostly uneventful. Very routine. Extremely ordinary.

But the Lord has asked us to rejoice always. He doesn't mean for us to wait for something big to happen and then rejoice. He means now. Right where you are. In your ordinary. In your routine. Maybe you are sitting with this book like me, wearing flip-flops, leaning back on my sofa, with clean hair but no make-up for days, khaki shorts, and a black T-shirt. Fancy, huh?

Right here. Right now. In your mundane and in mine, God is commanding us to choose joy. Will you spend these next moments with me rejoicing in your mundane. I'll start . . . you finish.

God, I praise you for the clean teacup that holds a breakfast blend. I rejoice in the hum of the air-conditioning that keeps me cool. I bless you for the gifts of laundry detergent, matching sheets, a satisfying granola bar, enough sleep . . .

....

....

....

TUESDAY

BE FAITHFUL IN THE LITTLE THINGS

God has this way of choosing very ordinary people to do great things. The youngest brother. Simple shepherds. An unmarried teenage girl. All through the Bible, God interrupts everyday people in the humdrum of life with His extraordinary assignments. But He does that when we have been faithful in the little things.

Remember the Master in the Parable of the Talents? He said, *"You have been faithful with a few things; I will put you in charge of many things"* (Matthew 25:23).

Our assignment every day is to be faithful in the few things and to rejoice always. In the routine. The repetitious. And even the wearisome.

Oh God, even if today is the most boring, routine, uneventful day ever, I want to rejoice! Let me be faithful in the smallest assignment. In the tiniest places, I give you praise!

What are the small assignments in your life that you may find wearisome? Are you being faithful with them?

....

....

....

WEDNESDAY
JUST BLESS GOD!

Look around the place you are sitting today and just bless God. Out loud. Find twenty reasons to praise Him, and write them down. Let your heart rejoice in all that is simple and plain and good.

....

....

....

THURSDAY
IT'S THE LITTLE MOMENTS THAT SHAPE US

"And we know that in all things God works for the good of those who love him, who have been called according to his purpose" (Romans 8:28). Maybe this year will contain three or four dramatic moments for you. More important, this year will probably have ten thousand little moments. You and I must remember that God is working in all of them. And probably, it's the little moments that will shape how we respond to the big ones.

I believe that moment by moment, little place to next little place, God is doing the slow and tedious work of refining our character. He is transforming us with little moments of grace and forgiveness. The change is almost imperceptible until the ten thousand are stacked together and you can see what God has done.

Let us choose joy today in the moment-by-moment work that God is doing to redeem our lives and shape our souls.

Look back upon the little moments God has used in the past. How has He done great things with the things that seemed so inconsequential at the time?

....

....

....

THE WEEKEND
ALL FOR THE GLORY OF GOD

"*So whether you eat or drink or whatever you do; do it all for the glory of God*" (1 Corinthians 10:31). Four things I ask the Lord this weekend:

1. *God, please* forgive *my disregard for the true joy found in the smallest things.*

2. *Lord, would you* heal *me and restore the joy of small treasures?*

3. *Father, give me eyes to* see *the small. I have too much been searching for the dramatic.*

4. *And God, please* deliver *me from any cynicism. Don't let boredom win my affection. Let me rejoice and be joyful always. In every small detail of this life on earth. Amen and amen.*

What are you asking the Lord this weekend?

....

....

....

For most of life, nothing wonderful happens. If you don't enjoy getting up and working and finishing your work and sitting down to a meal with family or friends, then the chances are that you're not going to be very happy. If someone bases his happiness or unhappiness on major events like a great new job, huge amounts of money, a flawlessly happy marriage, or a trip to Paris, that person isn't going to be happy much of the time. If, on the other hand, happiness depends on a good breakfast, flowers in the yard, a drink or a nap, then we are more likely to live with quite a bit of happiness.

—Andy Rooney

JOY

When You Are Weak

ALLOW YOUR REMORSE TO LEAD TO *STRENGTH*

"The joy of the LORD is your strength."
—Nehemiah 8:10

When Ezra the prophet arrived in Jerusalem, the spiritual condition of the people was reprehensible. But Ezra had been sent to teach the people God's Word. Nehemiah arrived a few years later and challenged the people to rebuild the walls of the city.

After the rebuilding, the people asked Ezra to continue teaching them the word of the Lord. Ezra stood on a platform above the people and read the Scriptures. The people's response to understanding God's Word was emotional. They lifted their hands, shouted "Amen!," bowed down, and worshipped the Lord they were beginning to understand. But the most powerful thing that happened was that as the people heard, they obeyed.

The Israelites wept, remorseful over their sins and past disobedience. But Nehemiah encouraged the people to consider that day sacred and to eat. They were to stop weeping, go home, give to others in need, and rejoice in the Lord, who was the source of their strength. The people were supposed to celebrate this new understanding of holiness with joy!

I'm imagining as they went home to prepare for their celebrations, the truth of what they had heard began to settle in their hearts: *God wants a relationship with people like us! He has promised to be our protector and our defender. He forgives us our sins. He is strong when we are weak.* What great joy must have welled up inside them as they understood the truths of God for the very first time. How overwhelming it must have been to receive an everlasting love they did not know belonged to them.

This week, my friend, let the truth of God's promises fall fresh on your weary heart. The joy of the Lord will be your strength. I pray that with each day, your heart will be strengthened. Your faith will be stirred. You will respond as the Israelites did. What are the promises of God in your life? Remind yourself of these and know that he is faithful.

....

....

....

TUESDAY
RUN TO GOD WITH YOUR SIN

God promises that He will forgive you of your sin. John tells us that *"If we confess our sins, he is faithful and just and will forgive us our sins and purify us from all unrighteousness"* (1 John 1:9).

Based on this verse, we should run. Flat out run to God

with every sin so that we can quickly be forgiven. The burden of sin makes you weak. The longer you carry it, the more discouraged you become. The more you endure it, the more you believe it to be unforgivable.

God forgives your sin. Let the joy of the promise fill your heart with strength today. Take some time to confess out loud, and write out the above verse to remind yourself of God's promise.

....

....

....

WEDNESDAY
THE JOY OF HIS PROMISE GIVES STRENGTH

"*All Scripture is God-breathed and is useful for teaching, rebuking, correcting and training in righteousness, so that the man of God may be thoroughly equipped for every good work*" (2 Timothy 3:16–17). The Word of God is so precious to me. It lays beside me right now turned to this underlined passage. I treasure even the very book I am privileged to hold in my hands. We are so very blessed to have been given the treasure of Scripture. We have only to read and obey. Study and apply. Receive and surrender. Hear and follow.

God has given us His Word to guide us. Let the joy of the promise fill your heart with strength today. Write out a prayer of thanksgiving to the Lord for the gift of His Word.

....

....

....

THURSDAY
RELAX IN GOD'S TIMING

"*Being confident of this, that he who began a good work in you will carry it on to completion until the day of Christ Jesus*" (Philippians 1:6). We are on a journey with the Lord. His timing is not ours. His purposes are so much greater than we can fathom. Let Him keep working out what He has begun in you. Give yourself to His shaping. Submit yourself to His tender guidance.

God will finish everything He has begun in you. Let the joy of the promise fill your heart with strength today. Have you believed that God will finish the work in you? How does your life reflect what you believe?

....

....

....

THE WEEKEND
STRENGTH TO THE WEARY

This morning, I can feel my weakness. It's been a long, exhausting week with lots of interactions with others and deadlines to meet. But deep inside of me I can rejoice. Isaiah reminds me that "*He gives strength to the weary and increases the power of the weak*" (40:29). God will provide the new strength that I need. The joy of the Lord will be my strength.

Maybe you need new strength this weekend, too. Will you take God at His word for a few days? Watch Him come to minister to you? Pay attention to how He puts His strength inside of you? Let the joy of the promise fill your heart with strength today. Take notes as to how God has increased your power when you were weak.

....

....

....

Trying to do the Lord's work in your own strength is the most confusing, exhausting, and tedious of all work. But when you are filled with the Holy Spirit, then the ministry of Jesus just flows out of you.

—*Corrie ten Boom*

In Obedience

"BE GENEROUS IN YOUR SURRENDER"

I rejoice in following your statutes as one rejoices in great riches.
—Psalm 119:14

Whoever has my commands and obeys them, he is the one who loves me.
He who loves me will be loved by my Father,
and I too will love him and show myself to him.
—John 14:21

This past year, the Lord has been forceful with me. I say forceful because He has been unrelenting with His message and the variety of messengers He has sent. He has been dealing with me about obedience. As far as I know, I am not making any disobedient choices, but I know the Lord is calling me to a deeper place of obedience. A deeper study of His Word. A greater dependence on the spirit. A richer fellowship with His body. Sweeter years with my family.

For most of my life, I have been following God as best as I knew how. But in these past months I am hearing Him say,

Come closer. Now that He has sent multiple messengers and many experiences to underscore His voice, I am standing at attention. My soul is eager. I am rejoicing that God is giving me instructions to obey.

I love what Hannah Whitall Smith writes in *The Christian's Secret of a Happy Life*:

> *Oh, be generous in your self-surrender! Meet His measureless devotion for you, with a measureless devotion to Him. Be glad and eager to throw yourself headlong into His dear arms, and to hand over the reins of government to Him. Whatever there is of you, let Him have it all. Give up forever everything that is separate from Him. Consent to resign from this time forward all liberty of choice; and glory in the blessed nearness of union which makes this enthusiasm of devotedness not only possible but necessary.*

This week we will choose the joy of obedience. There is delight in doing God's will. Joy in surrendering to His commands.

God has made me thirst for this kind of joy. I want the deeper places with God that will come from continued obedience. I pray for both of us that God will use this week to make us want Him more.

Would you begin with me in prayer and write out the rest?

Oh Lord, teach me to obey your commands, your direction, your instruction, your nudge and your shout. I love you.

....

....

....

⌒◦⌒ **TUESDAY** ⌒◦⌒
CHANGE OUR LAZY WAYS

"*I delight to do your will, O my God; your law is within my heart*" (Psalm 40:8, ESV). Delight is an eager joy! Have you been sluggish about obeying the Lord? Been dragging your feet about the very thing you know He has spoken to you? May the creator of our souls come and do a Holy Spirit work inside of us. May He forgive us for disobedience. Replace every hesitancy with eagerness. Change our lazy ways. Give us a craving for surrender.

Only the Lord can make the change that we need. Will you ask Him to work powerfully? Ask Him not to leave you alone.

....

....

....

⌒◦⌒ **WEDNESDAY** ⌒◦⌒
OBEY QUICKLY

"*We obey his commands and do what pleases him*" (1 John 3:22). Here is the deal about obedience to God. You cannot look from side to side to compare your own actions with what someone else is doing. Our responsibility in this life is to read His Word and quickly obey. That's it. You obey what the Lord reveals to you. Speaks to you. Shouts at you. Teaches you.

I want all of God's plan for *my* life. Every drop of it. Each time I stop to watch what someone else is doing or hasn't done, I'm wasting time. I'm wasting my calling. I'm slowing down my quick obedience.

Rejoice in what God has told someone else to do. Bless them. Pray for them. But be quick to do what He has shown you. What has God asked you to do today? Have you been dragging your feet and pointing at others?

....

....

....

THURSDAY

OBEDIENCE LEADS TO INTIMACY WITH GOD

As I hear the Lord saying to me "Come closer," it makes sense that deeper obedience is the path to greater intimacy. Jesus said, *"Obedience is thicker than blood. The person who obeys God's will is my brother and sister and mother"* (Mark 3:35, The Message). We are in the family. We are tight. Close-knit. Bonded.

Choose the joy of drawing closer to God in obedience. Has God been speaking to you this week? Has He highlighted a place where obedience is required?

....

....

....

THE WEEKEND
GOD BLESSES OUR OBEDIENCE

"*If you fully obey the LORD your God and carefully follow all his commands I give you today, the LORD your God will set you high above all the nations on earth. All these blessings will come upon you and accompany you if you obey the LORD your God*" (Deuteronomy 28:1–2). The Israelites were blessed for their obedience. Almost the entire book of Proverbs testifies that a life of obedience to God will be blessed.

For goodness sake, I want the blessing! God has wonderful things in store for those who keep His commands. We just need to take God at his word. I have known plenty of regret in my life so far, but the one thing I can say with complete assurance is that I have never, ever, not for a single second regretted obeying God.

I believe that God loves to pour out His blessing on the obedient because He gets the glory. This weekend, quickly obey God in all that He directs you to do.

You little know, dear hesitating soul, of the joy you are missing. The Master has revealed Himself to you, and is calling for your complete surrender, and you shrink and hesitate.
—*Hannah Whitall Smith*

In Knowing God More

MONDAY
KNOWING GOD THROUGH HIS SON JESUS

The life-maps of GOD are right, showing the way to joy.
The directions of GOD are plain and easy on the eyes.
—Psalm 19:8, The Message

We begin to know God when we first believe in Jesus Christ as our Savior. We will spend all of eternity growing in the knowledge of God. But on this earth, we can choose joy in knowing God more. Our joy will increase as we see His ways, understand His maps, and follow His directions. Spurgeon says, "The highest science, the loftiest speculation, the mightiest philosophy, which can ever engage the attention of a child of God, is the name, the nature, the person, the work, the doings, and the existence of the great God."

My goal this week is to introduce us to as many ways to know God as possible. There is a good possibility that I might miss something, so let your heart be open. May the Holy Spirit show you more than I have yet to understand.

Today let's begin with these. We can know God:

1. ***Through His Son,* Jesus Christ.** Christ is fully God in human flesh. Fully God on the cross. Fully God in the resurrection.

   - Write out John 14:6–7:...
   - *God, I want to know you more as I choose the joy of your Son, Jesus.*

2. ***Through the church.*** The church on this earth is the body of our Lord. We can know God more through His church. He is the head of the body, the church.

   - Write out Colossians 1:18:.............................
   - *God, I want to know you more as I choose the joy of belonging to your body, the church.*

3. ***Through His Word.*** The Bible contains the revelation of God. God does not think like us. He does not guide like us. We would do well to know Him more by studying all that He has revealed to us.

   - Write out Isaiah 55:8–9:.................................
   - *God, I want to know you more as I choose the joy of studying your Scriptures.*

This week, as we seek to know God more, I pray your soul will be stirred and your joy will increase. It is a privilege to seek for the Lord and find Him in so many ways.

TUESDAY
KNOWING GOD THROUGH WHAT HE HAS MADE

Today we continue with the ways we will know God more. We can know God:

4. ***Through His creation.***

- Write out Psalm 19:1–2: ....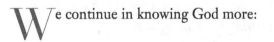
....

- Spend today knowing God more in His creation. Maybe you can catch only a glimpse through a window. Maybe there is time for a walk. Whatever you are given, open your eyes. What about creation helps you to know God more?
....

- *God, I want to know you more as I choose the joy of studying your creation.*

WEDNESDAY
KNOWING GOD THROUGH THE BEAUTY OF ART

We continue in knowing God more:

5. ***Through art.*** In my upbringing I was not exposed to the opportunity to know God through art; but in the past years, God has introduced me to His goodness in the gifts He has created through art. It's been said that ex-atheists have come to know God through the music

of Bach. They said that because of his glorious music, there must be a God.

Thankfully, God has birthed artists into my family and is teaching me to know Him more through the arts. Today, how will God reveal more of Himself to you in the mediums and expressions of art?

....

....

- *God, I want to know you more as I choose the joy of art.*

THURSDAY
KNOWING GOD THROUGH YOUR STORY

6. ***Through experience.*** You have a story, much of it still unwritten. In your story God is revealing His hand and his providence. He is teaching you more of Himself in the chapters that have been written. Through each plot line, twist, and climax, God is showing you more of His goodness. Will you look for Him in your story? Search for Him in your pages. What do you see?

....

....

- *God, I want to know you more as I choose the joy of experiencing you in my story.*

THE WEEKEND
KNOWING GOD THROUGH THE TESTIMONY
OF THE SAINTS

7. ***Through the testimony of the saints.*** God shows Himself in the lives of others. Those who have spent years in faithful obedience. Those who've been delivered from their consequences and pain. This weekend, why don't you spend some time with a saint? Let him tell you his story of God. Purpose in your heart to learn everything you can from his or her journey. Jot down notes on their story, so you can look back and remember later.

   ....

   ....

   ....

   • *God, I want to know you more as I choose the joy*
     of learning from your saints.

Disregard the study of God, and you sentence yourself to stumble and blunder through life blindfolded, as it were, with no sense of direction and no understanding of what surrounds you.
—*Charles Haddon Spurgeon*

In the Kingdom

MONDAY

KINGDOM JOY GIVES *EVERYTHING*

"The kingdom of heaven is like treasure hidden in a field.
When a man found it, he hid it again,
and then in his joy went and sold all he had and bought that field."
—Matthew 13:44

Seek first his kingdom and his righteousness
and all these things will be given to you as well.
—Matthew 6:33

Jesus told seven different parables about the kingdom in Matthew 13. This passionate parable is perhaps one of the most stirring illustrations of what joy will do. Joy will make a plan. Joy will sell everything. Joy will work to possess the object and the source of its delight. Joy over the kingdom of heaven is life changing.

The kingdom of heaven refers to God's dominion in Christ. God's kingly rule through Christ. The kingdom of heaven is here on this earth and also in heaven. God's rule is recognized by God's people, and to belong to the kingdom of heaven is the great privilege for all who believe in Christ. One day, all nations and all people will recognize God and be ruled by the authority of His kingdom.

I love that Jesus paints a picture of joy when he is describing the kingdom. I can see the man in my head. I hear his glee over finding the treasure. I watch him bury the treasure until he can do whatever it takes to possess it. I can feel the joy that motivates him to work so hard. And his great delight when the treasure is his.

Do you know this kind of life-stirring joy? Maybe you are like me, and this very day you need a fresh indwelling of this passionate kingdom joy. I'm worn out from a hundred good things. My soul reads this passage and wants to be the man jumping up and down in a field, but I am not. On the inside, my heart rejoices, but my physical body needs a nap. And so I'm asking the Lord to inspire us both. I'll start, and you finish:

God, would you let the great kingdom joy become mine anew this week. In all of us, breathe new strength so that we might live this kind of joy with greater passion and vitality. Let us rejoice body, soul, and mind over the treasure we have received in Christ Jesus.

....

....

....

TUESDAY
KINGDOM TREASURE CAN NEVER BE STOLEN

As we spend this week focused on the kingdom, take a look at the next parable Jesus told: " *'Again, the kingdom of heaven is like a merchant looking for fine pearls. When he found one of great value, he went away and sold everything he had and bought it' "* (Matthew 13:45–46).

In the first parable, Jesus calls the kingdom a treasure hidden in a field. In this parable, the kingdom is likened to a merchant looking for fine pearls. A treasure or pearls, Jesus gives two different illustrations because he wants to communicate the great value of the kingdom.

I can get so busy focusing on my earthly needs and organizing my earthly stuff that I forget I am rich. We set a security alarm when we leave our house to protect our things. But God has given me a treasure that will never be stolen. We belong to the kingdom. The great treasure of Christ is ours.

Have you taken the great value of the kingdom for granted? Take a moment to give thanks.

....

....

....

WEDNESDAY
GOD'S KINGDOM IS WORTH *ALL* WE HAVE

When the man in the field and the merchant hunting for a pearl found treasure, they both sold everything to get it. Jesus says that's how we should act about the kingdom. The point with these parables is not that the kingdom is bought. The point is that the kingdom is worth everything we have.

Notice in the first parable that the man sold everything he had and he did it with great joy. The kingdom of God is so valuable that losing everything to acquire it is a happy trade-off. I don't think we have to run out and sell everything today. That's not the idea. But do you regard the kingdom of God as more valuable than all that you have?

....

....

....

Paul knew the value of the kingdom when he wrote, *"But whatever was to my profit I now consider loss for the sake of Christ"* (Philippians 3:7). It's kingdom thinking and a kingdom heart that Jesus wants.

THURSDAY
YOUR HEART FOLLOWS YOUR TREASURE

"*What is more, I consider everything a loss compared to the surpassing greatness of knowing Christ Jesus my Lord, for whose sake I have lost all things. I consider them rubbish, that*

I may gain Christ and be found in him, not having a righteousness of my own that comes from the law, but that which is through faith in Christ—the righteousness that comes from God and is by faith" (Philippians 3:8–9).

God wants us to receive the kingdom of heaven and value it more than anything. We receive it freely. It costs us nothing, and yet we are to want it more than all else. Jesus also said, *"Where your treasure is, there your heart will be also"* (Matthew 6:21).

Your heart follows your treasure. Have you made a kingdom adjustment about what you treasure most? What, if anything, is holding you back? Determine the kingdom is more valuable than all, and your heart will follow your decision.

....

....

....

THE WEEKEND
GOD'S KINGDOM *REQUIRES* SOMETHING OF YOU

When we begin to treasure the kingdom of heaven above all else, then our priorities begin to change.

> We long for others to have the same joy for the kingdom that we have been given.

> We become the hands and feet of Christ to work in His kingdom.

> We invest our money and our time for the spread of the kingdom.

This weekend, choose the joy of the kingdom. What is God asking you to do with your treasure?

....

....

....

If you have not chosen the Kingdom of God first, it will in the end make no difference what you have chosen instead.

—*William Law*

WEEK 50

In Sorrow

JOY WILL SURELY BE WOVEN WITH SORROW

*Sorrowful, yet always **rejoicing**.*
—2 Corinthians 6:10

Just as it is assigned for us to live on this earth, there is surely an assignment that we all will endure times of sorrow. Our immediate family has known deep days of sorrow. The drowning of my sister. The tragic loss of my aunt in a plane crash.

It is amazing how vividly I can recall the emotion of sorrow after writing only a few sentences of remembrance. Sorrow consumes you. The images of its presence burn themselves into your soul. Quiet weeping in every room. Hushed whispers of condolence. The sound of food being delivered in the kitchen. Aluminum foil being torn to cover the leftovers. The tragically long, dark nights. The great grief that a new day has come and the sorrow remains.

I lost my baby sister thirty-five years ago. Thirty-five years. How in the world can that sorrow resurrect itself with only a thought? She would have been thirty-seven this summer. She would have been cute and beautiful and fun. Much more fun than me. She was the baby of four children. I was the oldest. How I wish she was here to be my best friend. I miss the grown-up her I never knew.

As I remember my loss, my broken heart clings to this one thing: God is not almost sovereign. He *is* sovereign in all things. He did not look away when my sister ran into the water.

We've spent all these weeks together intentionally focusing our lives on the pursuit of joy. But while we are on this earth, the joy we pursue and the joy we embrace in Jesus Christ will always be interwoven with sorrow. The Bible describes the followers of Christ as *"sorrowful but always rejoicing."* I am sure that you already know that to be true.

Life is not simple. There will be pleasure and pain. Sweetness and suffering. Rejoicing and sorrow. And for the follower of Christ, it means there will be times we *"rejoice with those who rejoice and weep with those who weep"* (Romans 12:15, ESV).

God's answer to all of our sorrow was the suffering and death of His Son: *"Surely he took up our infirmities and carried our sorrows"* (Isaiah 53:4).

Jesus came to this fallen world and took the full weight of our sorrow to the cross. By his death, the cure for our sorrow—forgiveness and everlasting life—has come. That is why, as Christians, we can be sorrowful yet always rejoicing.

Is your rejoicing woven with sorrow today?

....

....

....

❦ **TUESDAY** ❦
THE HOLY COMFORTER

J esus knew the sorrows of this world, the scorn, rejection, suffering, and even death. But Jesus did not leave us without a Holy Comfort. The night of his betrayal, Jesus promised to send his disciples the Holy Spirit, who is our comforter. *"And I will pray to the Father, and he shall give you another Comforter, that he may be with you for ever"* (John 14:16, ASV).

The Comforter lives inside of you. Ministering in your sorrows. Reminding you to always rejoice. Pointing you toward our great hope in heaven. Will you let the Comforter minister to you today? I'll start, and you write out the rest of the prayer.

Come, sweet Holy Spirit, and minister the comfort of your indwelling. Make alive in me a spirit of rejoicing even though this world is filled with sorrow.

....

....

....

❦ **WEDNESDAY** ❦
SORROW WILL NOT CONSUME US

W e will each have to experience sorrow on this earth, but oh, hallelujah, it cannot consume us. Sorrow will not last forever. An end will come. A morning will break, and joy will shout!

Maybe today you are walking through a valley of shadow. Maybe your heart is full of sorrow. Oh, my friend, keep walking. One small step of faith in front of another. Walk through that valley. You do not have to live there.

If you are too tired for the next step, would you reach out to the body of Christ? They have been charged with the joy of carrying one another's burdens. This may be your time to be carried. Find Psalm 30:5 in your Bible and write out that verse below.

Be encouraged.

....

....

....

THURSDAY

HEAVEN'S PROMISE—NO MORE SORROW

"*So with you: Now is your time of grief, but I will see you again and you will rejoice, and no one will take away your joy*" (John 16:22). Every time I remember that I am going home, I feel a flutter of joy inside. One day, I will stand in front of my Savior and He will wipe my tears, once and for all. There will be no more sorrow for this old soul of mine. My joy will not be woven with sorrow anymore. All things will be new and pure delight will be ours.

Do you have tears in your eyes today? Write out Revelation 21:4, and carry that promise with you today.

....

....

....

THE WEEKEND
ONE DAY

Maybe Jesus wants to tell you today:

I see your sorrow. I have felt your pain. But I want you to know that one day you will understand. One day you will see the fruit of your life on this earth, and your grief will turn to joy. You will see what I have done, and you will declare that it was all worth it. The joy you will know will wipe away every memory of your sorrow. One day, this pain will seem like a dream. Distant. Far away. Healed. Redeemed.

Maybe this weekend, God wants to send you to be comfort and joy for someone. Would you listen for Him to tell you who? What if you don't know what to say or how to give comfort for someone else's sorrow? You can begin with these words: *Hello friend, I'm here to cry with you . . .*

Write down the people God brings to mind.

....

....

....

Shared joy is double joy; shared sorrow is half a sorrow.
—*Swedish proverb*

In Response to Our Blessings

⤸⤷⤸ **MONDAY** ⤸⤷⤸

OUR HISTORY OF JOY

When the LORD brought back the captives to Zion,
we were like men who dreamed.
Our mouths were filled with laughter,
*our tongues with songs of **joy**.*
Then it was said among the nations,
"The LORD has done great things for them."
*The LORD has done great things for us, and we are filled with **joy**.*
Restore our fortunes, O LORD,
like streams in the Negev.
Those who sow in tears
*will reap with songs of **joy**.*
He who goes out weeping,
carrying seed to sow,
*will return with songs of **joy**,*
carrying sheaves with him.
—Psalm 126

By now you know that we cannot force ourselves to be joyful. We can't command joy. Or buy joy. Or make some arrangements that produce joy. It just can't be done.

But there is something we can do. We can choose. We can choose to respond to God's abundance instead of focusing on what else we want. We can center our decisions, intentions, and choices on the very person of God, not allowing our greediness to lead. When we choose joy as the response to our blessings, we will certainly be living as God intended.

Solomon wrote Psalm 126 in response to the blessings of everyday lives. The domestic life. And so it seems fitting for us to spend a week with this psalm, learning to choose joy in the blessings of our everyday.

Let's jump right into the middle of the passage at verse 3, *"We are filled with joy."*

The verses before this line look back to the past. And the next verses talk about present and future gladness. Solomon isn't writing about a really great day he just had or good news that gave him a shot of joy; his writing is spread across a lifetime.

First, Solomon remembers that his people have been blessed by God. Their joy has a history. Their story is full of His abundant provision. His deliverance. God parted the seas for these people, and Solomon remembers the laughter and the songs when their hearts were filled with joy.

I bet your joy has a history, too. Take a few minutes to reflect on your joy history with God. Like the psalmist, how can you say, "The Lord has done great things for us"? List your top three memories.

1. ....

2. ....

3. ....

In light of your past joy, how can you trust God for joy even when your soul feels dry?

....

....

....

❧❧❧ **TUESDAY** ❧❧❧
TRUSTING GOD FOR FUTURE JOY

On the other side of *"we are filled with joy,"* in Psalm 126, Solomon looks toward the future. Because of their joy history with God, the people look toward the future with joyful anticipation. They have known the joy God produced in their past, so they turn and trust Him for their future. The Lord says, " *'I the LORD do not change'* " (Malachi 3:6).

We can have the same expectation as Solomon. There is no reason that God is going to suddenly stop working as He always has. God had produced joy in the past. Solomon could trust Him for joy in the future.

Do you need to trust God for your future joy? Be reminded that He has not changed. He is still the God of your story. The giver of your blessings. The reason for our joy. Write out a prayer of thanksgiving in faith for your future joy.

....

....

....

WEDNESDAY
A FRESH RAIN

"*Restore our fortunes, O LORD, like streams in the Negev*" (Psalm 126:4). The Negev is a desert, dry and barren most of the time, but a sudden rain will set the desert alive with blooms. Solomon asked the Lord for joy like streams in the Negev.

The Message paraphrases, "*And now, GOD, do it again—* bring rains to our drought-stricken lives."

Does your soul feel drought stricken? Do you need fresh rain? Pray this passage just like Solomon did. Pray over your heart. Pray for your marriage. Pray for your home. Pray for your work. Just stop and ask God to do it again. Ask God to interrupt your drought with His grace.

....

....

....

THURSDAY
A HARVEST OF JOY

"*Those who sow in tears will reap with songs of joy. He who goes out weeping, carrying seed to sow, will return with songs of joy, carrying sheaves with him*" (Psalm 126:5–6). Farmers know this picture. They sow seeds in the fertile earth and reap a blessing at harvest. Solomon says that we sow our pain. We sow our disappointment. We sow our tears and watch God bring the harvest of joy.

I think that picture is beautiful. My tears, my weeping, my troubles all sown into the fertile ground of God. And then God, in His divine power, is able to work all those things for good to bring a crop of joy.

When I think about it, what better place for my sorrow and my disappointment? I will plant them all with God, anticipating that because God is God, I will return with songs of joy. Take some time to honestly talk to God about your pain and disappointment. Lay it all at his feet, and listen for his comfort and songs of joy.

....

....

....

THE WEEKEND
A TESTIMONY OF JOY

Psalm 126 is not a formula for joy; it's a testimony. Six verses remind us that we trade in our everyday sorrows with the Lord, trusting Him to bring the harvest of joy. He delivers the slaves from captivity. He brings the rain to the drought stricken.

God's work of abundance in our lives is supposed to put laughter in our mouth and songs in our heart. God is with us, testifies this psalm, walking with us through the planting of tears until we arrive at the harvest with "armloads of blessing."

Looking back at your joy history and forward to God's unchanging promises, you and I are supposed to live this day "filled with joy." Joy lies ahead for all of us, and we can choose joy today because of it.

This weekend, tell someone else about the promised joy they can count on with God. Write out a testimony from your life in preparation.

....

....

....

When was the last time you laughed for the sheer joy of your salvation?
—Anonymous

So That I Bear Fruit

MONDAY
DON'T LEAVE ANY JOY ON THE TABLE

So, I say, live by the Spirit.
—Galatians 5:16

*But the fruit of the Spirit is love, **joy**, peace, patience, kindness,
goodness, faithfulness, gentleness and self-control.*
—Galatians 5:22–23

I chose you and appointed you so that you would go and bear fruit.
—John 15:16, NASB

After months of intense word study, hours and hours of reading, prayers, headaches, and physical weariness, I can tell you this: my pursuit of joy has made me long for joy all the more. Choosing joy has taken its place among my highest spiritual priorities.

The Bible calls us into a joy-filled life so that we might do several things:

- Bring glory to God.
- Draw others toward the saving grace of Jesus Christ.
- Minister to the body of Christ.
- Be well equipped to deal with life's ups and downs.

The pursuit of joy is an act of obedience. Choosing joy is a mark of spiritual maturity. The fullness of joy is given by the Holy Spirit who lives in us. And I want the fullness. All these months of studying have underscored one thing for me personally: I don't want to leave any joy on the table. I don't want to get to heaven and have God say to me, "Welcome home, good and faithful servant. Oh, and by the way, you missed so much joy. The Spirit was ready to pour it out, but you missed it."

Galatians 5:22 is very clear. Joy is a fruit of the Spirit. Joy is produced by the Holy Spirit in my character and in yours. I can choose joy with my mind and move toward joy in my choices, but a character filled with joy has the Holy Spirit working inside producing fruit.

So the theological issue and the very personal issue is this: will I live in such a way, surrendered to the Holy Spirit, so that the Spirit is free to fill me and keep refilling me with joy? And with everything inside of me, I am yelling, *YES! I want to be a fruit grower. Fertile ground. Gates of my garden wide open. Heart ready and willing. Yes, Lord, yes, fill my life with fruit!*

This week let's look at the characteristics of a life that bears fruit. Each day, we'll tackle a new thought. Each day I pray you'll take that nugget and apply it to your life.

Today let's begin with the invitation. Would you invite the Holy Spirit to grow the beautiful fruit of His Spirit inside of you? Pray as you are led, but open the gates of your life, your mind, your home, your choices. Let the Spirit in.

....

....

....

⊙ ✺ⁿ⊙ TUESDAY ⊙ ✺ⁿ⊙
EXALT THE NAME OF JESUS

"*While Peter was still speaking these words, the Holy Spirit came on all who heard the message*" (Acts 10:44). Several times in the book of Acts we read about the Holy Spirit joining people who were lifting up the name of Jesus. Teaching and preaching the truths of Jesus. It seems like the Spirit likes to be where Jesus is being exalted.

We are choosing the joy that comes from fruit when we make everyday choices to exalt the name of Jesus. I want my home to be a haven of grace, testifying to the matchless name of Jesus. My choices. My reactions. My service. The care of my physical body.

Does your life exalt Jesus? The Holy Spirit likes to work in an environment like that. What can you do to make your home a place of praise that invites the Holy Spirit?

....

....

....

WEDNESDAY
CHECK THE GARDEN OF YOUR SOUL

I have a little flower garden out back, and unless I am diligent, it can quickly become a weed patch. It's the same with our souls. To remain fertile soil for fruit growing, we must be diligent to keep ourselves clean. We must regularly go to the Lord and ask Him if there is anything hindering the growth of spiritual fruit.

In my backyard, I love to grab those little weeds and yank them from the ground while they are just beginning to take root. It's so much easier when they are small. It's the same with our sin. Yank that sin early. When it's tiny. Before the roots have gone down deep.

"If we confess our sins, he is faithful and just to forgive us our sins and to cleanse us from all unrighteousness" (1 John 1:9, ESV). Check the garden of your soul today. Look for tiny weeds that have crept in. Then take God at His word and ask Him to make you clean.

....

....

....

THURSDAY
DAILY REMINDERS TO SURRENDER

I hope I'm not sounding like a nutcase, but this commitment to "live by the Spirit" has become really important to me. I have proven that I lack the power of determination. I can't last very long on my own willpower. I want a live-by-the-Spirit, bearing-all-the-fruit-I-can kind of life!

Every morning, before I get out of bed, I begin to pray,

Lord, fill me again. Keep me full of your Spirit today. Let my mind be sensitive to the Spirit. I want to know what life looks like when I am moving fully in the power of your Spirit. Let the fruit grow in me!

I have to remind myself to surrender, and that morning prayer seems to be the best reminder for me. How will you remind yourself to cooperate with the Holy Spirit? A note on your mirror? An alarm on your cell phone? A visual sitting on your desk?

....

....

....

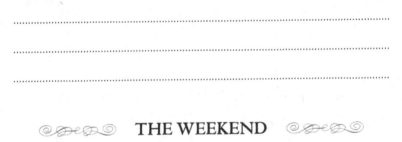

THE WEEKEND

SHARE YOUR FRUIT!

"*By this My Father is glorified, that you bear much fruit*" (John 15:8, ESV). I don't think that the Holy Spirit produces the fruit of joy in your character just for you to sit at home and look at your joy. I believe the Lord means for you to get out there and share your fruit! For goodness sake, this world needs joy to show up!

Where will you show up with your joy this weekend? What commitment will you make to share your fruit?

....

....

....

Go get 'em, my friend . . . it is to your Father's glory that you bear much fruit!

It is the consciousness of the threefold joy of the LORD, His joy in ransoming us, His joy in dwelling within us as our Savior and Power for fruitbearing and His joy in possessing us, as His Bride and His delight; it is the consciousness of this joy which is our real strength.

—*James Hudson Taylor,*
James Hudson Taylor Biography

Acknowledgments

My first thanks goes to my editor at Howard Books, Philis Boultinghouse, one of the most kind and gentle women I've ever known. Philis, this whole book takes it shape and direction from your great idea. You were able to take one little thought and grow it into a year-long devotional. Thank you for all the calls and encouraging e-mails as we sought the Lord together for these words.

Thanks to the rest of my team at Howard: Jonathan Merkh, Jessica Wong, and Nancy Inglis. It has been such a pleasure to work with you all.

Here in the office, I'm so very grateful to Lisa Stridde, Carla Lake, and Lynn Ransom for holding all the details together.

At home, I have to thank my ever-cheering kids: Anna-Grace, William, Grayson, and Taylor. You give me such great ideas, stories, and inspiration. Thanks to my parents, Joe and Novie Thomas; my new parents, Walt and Faye Pharr; and all the rest of our beautiful family and friends. My special thanks to my husband, Scott. You are unwavering in your belief in me.

Your love gives me such strength and, many days, a soft place to fall. Thank you for putting me in a beautiful hotel room to finish this book and then blessing all the time that it took me to write.

And to Jesus, I am so grateful that you sat me down and gave me this special assignment called joy. May all that I have written, and especially the way I live my life, reflect the pursuit of joy You have placed in my heart.

Notes

Week 1: Joy . . . for the Glory of God

1. Saint Augustine, *Confessions* X, 22.

Week 3: Joy . . . Defined

1. R. L. Pratt, Jr., *Holman New Testament Commentary: Volume 7, 1 & 2 Corinthians* (Nashville, TN: Broadman & Holman Publishers, 2000), p. 447.
2. M. H. Manser, *Zondervan Dictionary of Bible Themes: The Accessible and Comprehensive Tool for Topical Studies* (Grand Rapids, MI: Zondervan Publishing House, 1999).
3. C. Brand, C. Draper, A. England, et al., *Holman Illustrated Bible Dictionary* (Nashville, TN: Holman Bible Publishers, 2003), p. 956.
4. D. A. Carson, *New Bible Commentary: 21st Century Edition*, 4th ed. (Leicester, England; Downers Grove, IL: Inter-Varsity Press, 1994), 1 Thessalonians 5:12–24.
5. W. A. Elwell and P. W. Comfort, *Tyndale Bible Dictionary* (Wheaton, IL: Tyndale House Publishers, 2001), p. 745.

Week 6: Joy . . . Given by God

1. John Piper, *When I Don't Desire God: How to Fight for Joy* (Pelham, AL: Crossway Books, 2008), from the foreword.

Week 12: Joy . . . in the Presence of God

1. Richard Foster, *Celebration of Discipline* (San Francisco: HarperSan-Francisco, 1988), p. 30.
2. Ibid., p. 19.
3. Ibid., p. 76.

Week 42: Joy . . . in Gratitude

1. John Piper, sermon entitled "Grace, Gratitude and the Glory of God." Thanksgiving 1981, desiringgod.com.

Week 44: Joy . . . in Friendship and Hospitality

1. P. L. Tan, *Encyclopedia of 7700 Illustrations: Signs of the Times* (Garland, TX: Bible Communications, Inc., 1996).

Journaling Pages for Your *Joyful* Journey

Journaling Pages for Your *Joyful* Journey

....

....

....

....

....

....

....

....

....

....

....

....

....

....

....

....

....

....

....

Journaling Pages for Your *Joyful* Journey

....

....

....

....

....

....

....

....

....

....

....

....

....

....

....

....

....

....

Journaling Pages for Your *Joyful* Journey

....

....

....

....

....

....

....

....

....

....

....

....

....

....

....

....

....

....

....

Journaling Pages for Your *Joyful* Journey

....
....
....
....
....
....
....
....
....
....
....
....
....
....
....
....
....
....
....
....
....

Journaling Pages for Your *Joyful* Journey

....
....
....
....
....
....
....
....
....
....
....
....
....
....
....
....
....
....
....
....
....
....

Journaling Pages for Your *Joyful* Journey

....
....
....
....
....
....
....
....
....
....
....
....
....
....
....
....
....
....

Journaling Pages for Your *Joyful* Journey

....
....
....
....
....
....
....
....
....
....
....
....
....
....
....
....
....
....
....
....
....
....

Journaling Pages for Your *Joyful* Journey

Journaling Pages for Your *Joyful* Journey

....

....

....

....

....

....

....

....

....

....

....

....

....

....

....

....

....

....

....